ADOLF HITLER
EVOLUTION
OF A DICTATOR

ADOLF HITLER

EVOLUTION
OF A DICTATOR

Text by Luciano and Simonetta Garibaldi

WHITE STAR PUBLISHERS

WHITE STAR PUBLISHERS

WS White Star Publishers® is a registered trademark
property of De Agostini Libri S.p.A.

© 2014 De Agostini Libri S.p.A.
Via G. da Verrazano, 15
28100 Novara, Italy
www.whitestar.it - www.deagostini.it

Translation: Catherine Bolton
Editing: Richard Pierce

ISBN 978-88-544-0897-5
1 2 3 4 5 6 18 17 15 14

Printed in Poland

A portrait of Hitler by his personal photographer Heinrich Hoffmann. The photo was ▶
*taken in 1928, when the future dictator had gained a major electoral success. His
greatest strength was his violent oratory, which captivated the public. Soon afterward he
would wear the Nazi uniform.*

4

Contents

Introduction

Hitler, Nazism and the Third Reich are three 20th-century realities that will never fail to intrigue us. Virtually every day the media reports and comments on the events, stories and persons related to Nazism. Recently a sensational discovery was made in Munich – what the world press has described as "Hitler's treasure": approximately 1500 works of art, including paintings by such masters as Picasso, Matisse, Renoir and Chagall, which were hidden in an apartment belonging to the 80 year-old son of an art dealer who had bought the works that high-ranking Nazi officials had confiscated from Jewish families or from museums in Nazi-occupied Europe during the war. These artworks are worth 1 billion euro. Again, various European countries, from Greece to Norway, have witnessed the rise of extremist right-wing organizations (the one in Athens is called Golden Dawn) that quite openly exhibit their nostalgia and admiration for Hitler's policies. In Italy as well, the 2013 death of former SS captain Erich Priebke – one of those responsible for the execution (known as the Adreatine Cave reprisal) of 335 persons as retaliation for a partisan attack against the German troops in Italy – triggered violent, often excessive polemics from both those who continued to justify the Nazi reprisal and those

Adolf Hitler in 1936, the year that sealed the fate of Germany (and Europe) after the ▶ signing of the Pact of Steel with Fascist Italy and the Anti-Comintern Pact with Japan.

who vigorously upheld the view that Priebke did not deserve a regular funeral.

Then there is the phenomenon of historical revisionism, especially that concerning the death of Hitler and his companion Eva Braun. The number of persons who do not believe the couple committed suicide in Hitler's Berlin bunker is steadily increasing. Gerard Williams and Simon Dunstan, the British authors of Grey Wolf: the Escape of Adolf Hitler, *steadfastly maintain that the couple escaped to South America and settled in Argentine Patagonia. They claim that the former Führer died of cerebral hemorrhage on February 13, 1962, leaving Eva Braun to take care of their two daughters. The most convinced and tenacious Italian supporter of the Argentine hypothesis is Professor Alessandro De Felice, the cousin of the famous historian of Fascism, who illustrated the results of his research in a long and detailed interview that he granted to Stefano Lorenzetto and that was published in the Italian daily paper* Il Giornale *on May 20, 2012. Another history researcher in Italy deeply involved in this question is Giorgio Vitali, according to whom Hitler secured his safety and escape by 'bribing' half the secret service agencies in the world, which were pursuing him, with securities from the Reichsbank, the Central German Bank (as well as some from the Central Bank of Italy). Are these merely storybook theories with a kernel of truth? Whatever the case, they have attracted the interest of popular TV programs, such as Roberto Giacobbo's* Voyager, *broadcast in Italy in May 2010.*

What is indisputable is that too much has been written and said about Hitler and Nazism, often without any knowledge of their ideology, what they were and what they did. Hence the publication of this book, a work I have thought about for years, even decades, as is normal for anyone like myself who was born in the 1930s. The desire to delve into and relate the story of Hitler and the Third Reich became stronger when, way back in 1964, on the occasion of the 20th anniversary of the abortive July 20, 1944 assassination attempt, I spent more than a month in Germany interviewing the conspirators who had survived, using the material gathered for a series of articles published in various Italian daily newspapers, material that was the nucleus of my book Operazione Walkiria. Hitler deve morire *(Operation Valkyrie. Hitler Must Die; Ares Publishers, 'Faretra series', 2008). And so we now have this history of the Third Reich, which I have written together with my daughter Simonetta, who is also a passionate history researcher.*

The criterion we have followed is the most natural one, based on the chronology of the events, which is the most popular approach among average readers. Thus, our narrative unfolds with the various stages of the life — not only political and public, but also private and intimate — of Adolf Hitler, and at the same time the tragedy that in a few years overwhelmed Germany, Europe and the whole world. It is as if the reader had two books in one: an in-depth biography of the protagonist on the one hand, and the history of the Third Reich and the political, military and even religious history of the major events that occurred in the twelve years of the 'Thousand-year Reich', on the other.

The account begins with Hitler's family, his childhood and his studies at Braunau and Linz and the troubled period of the would-be artist in Vienna. It goes on to describe his experience at the front during World War One, the discovery in Munich of his political vocation, and the exaltation of violence as a tool to conquer power. Then there is Hitler's Mein Kampf *and a thorough description of how he put the ideas of this book into practice by rearming Germany, initiating political and military aggression that led to the outbreak of World War Two. The events of the war led to the apocalyptic end of the Nazi regime in the Berlin bunker and the Nuremberg trial, which was the modern-day version of the Latin saying* vae victis *(woe to the vanquished). We have availed ourselves of all the historic sources that would help us under-stand the psychology and nature of a man who prompted the suicide of all the women who fell in love with him and who had around 5000 of the most highly regarded officers in his army hanged because they had dared to oppose his tryanny.*

Our aim has been objectivity, which consists in not omitting any-thing regarding the criminal acts of the Third Reich and its Führer – first and foremost the horrendous persecution of the Jewish people – while at the same keeping Hitler's private life within the bounds of credibility, without excess or facile stigmatization, such as his alleged homosexuality.

A final comment: we have read and taken into account all the principal works written about this subject (indeed, one section of the Appendix features the opinions of the leading historians of Nazism, such as Raymond Cartier, Lord Russell, William Shirer, Joachim Fest and Alan Bullock), including private writings such as the memoirs of Hitler's secretary Traudl Junge, who died in 2002, and Hitler's Second Book: The Unpublished Sequel to Mein Kampf, *published the following year in New York by Enigma Books, which has also pub-lished one of my books.*

Luciano Garibaldi
December 2013

1938: in the mythical Nuremberg stadium, which hosted the annual Parteitag or ▶
National Socialist Party Congress, thousands of uniformed Hitler Youth (Hitlerjugend)
welcome the Führer.

Chronology

• *9 November 1918:* Wilhelm II renounces the Prussian crown. The Social Democrat Scheidemann proclaims the birth of the Republic.

• *5 January 1919:* Anton Drexler founds the German Workers Party.

• *10 July 1921:* Hitler becomes head of Drexler's party, now renamed National Socialist German Workers Party.

• *8-9 November 1923:* the so-called Beer Hall Putsch in Munich planned by the National Socialists is a failure.

• *1 April 1924:* Hitler sentenced to a five-year prison term but is set free after only 9 months. While in the Landsberg prison he dictates his *Mein Kampf* to Rudolph Hess.

• *20 December 1924:* Hitler leaves prison.

• *27 February 1925:* the National Socialist party is reestablished and that same year takes part in the national election, with very disappointing results.

• *6 May 1928:* the National Socialist Party obtains 2.6% of the votes.

• *14 September 1930:* the National Socialist Party obtains 18.3% of the votes, earning 107 seats in Parliament compared to the 77 of the Communists.

• *March-April 1932:* in the following two elections Hitler obtains 30.1% and 36.8% of the vote. Hindenburg wins the elections.

• *6 November 1932:* the National Socialist Party drops to 33.1% of the total vote.

• *30 January 1933:* Hindenburg makes Adolf Hitler the Chancellor. This marks the end of the Weimar Republic.

• *27 February 1933:* the Reichstag is burned down. Hitler accuses the Communists and enacts the first repressive laws, which suspend the political rights guaranteed by the German Constitution.

• *5 March 1933:* in a climate of terror and intimidation, the Nationalist Socialist Party wins the elections and enacts the Enabling Act, which gives Hitler total power, thus eliminating parliamentary legislation.

• *21 March 1933:* creation of the *Volksgerichtshof* or People's Court.

• *22 March 1933:* the concentration camp of Dachau is created to house political opponents.

• *23 March 1933:* the Reichstag grants Hitler total power.

• *1 April 1933:* boycott of all Jewish businesses.

• *7-12 April 1933:* enactment of the first anti-Jewish legislation: Jews are barred from civil service and skilled occupations.

• *26 April 1933:* establishment of the Gestapo (*Geheime Staats Polizei*), the German secret police.

• *10 May 1933:* books written by Jews and opponents of Nazism are burned at the University of Berlin.

• *14 July 1933:* the National Socialist Party is the only political organization allowed in Germany.

• *3 October 1933:* Germany abandons the League of Nations and the World Disarmament Conference in Geneva. The country is now totally 'isolated' from the rest of the world.

• *30 June 1934:* the *Langmessernacht* or Night of the Long Knives: Ernst Röhm and the leaders of the SA (*Sturmabteilung*, known in

English as the Brownshirts) are massacred in a dramatic bloodbath planned by Hitler and carried out by his faithful SS (*Schutz Staffeln* or protection squadrons).

• *2 August 1934:* President Hindenburg dies. Hitler becomes both Chancellor and President of the Republic. The Armed Forces no longer swear loyalty to the Head of State, but to Hitler himself.

• *15 September 1935:* the anti-Semitic Nuremberg laws are enacted.

• *7 March 1936:* German troops occupy the Rhineland, which had been demilitarized by the Versailles Treaty. This marks the end of the agreements made at the end of the Great War.

• *17 June 1936:* Heinrich Himmler is named supreme head of all the German police corps.

• *23 October 1936:* the alliance pact between Fascist Italy and Nazi Germany (the Rome-Berlin Axis) is signed. This is followed in November by the Anti-Comintern (anti-communist) Pact, which marks the beginning of German-Japanese collaboration against the Soviet Union.

• *16 July 1937:* establishment of the Buchenwald concentration camp.

• *13 March 1938:* the *Anschluss*: Austria is annexed into the Third Reich.

• *14 March 1938:* with the *'Mit brennender Sorge'* (With Burning Concern) encyclical, Pope Pius XI takes a stand against Nazis and denounces Hitler's violations of the concordat between Germany and the Catholic Church.

• *9 June 1938:* the Munich synagogue is destroyed.

• *10 August 1938:* the Nuremberg synagogue is destroyed.

• *30 September 1938:* at the Munich Conference (participants: Italy, Germany, France and Great Britain), promoted by Mussolini to avoid a war, it is agreed that the Sudetenland be ceded to Germany.

ADOLF HITLER

EVOLUTION
OF A DICTATOR

• *9 September 1943:* after the Italian government, now headed by Marshal Badoglio, signs an armistice with the Allies, the Germans invade Italy and rescue Mussolini, who then creates the Italian Social Republic.

• *6 June 1944:* the Allies land in Normandy. Two days earlier they take Rome, forcing the German troops to retreat behind the Gothic Line.

• *20 July 1944:* failed assassination attempt against Hitler at Rastenburg, organized by some leaders of the German Armed Forces and carried out by Colonel Claus von Stauffenberg. Thousands of persons are condemned to death and hanged.

• *1 August 1944:* insurrection in Warsaw on the part of the Armija Krajowa, made up of volunteers. It is cruelly suppressed, partly because the Russians, who arrive as far as the city gates, refuse to support the rebels.

• *16 December 1944:* desperate German counterattack in the Ardennes, known as Hitler's 'Watch on the Rhine'.

• *27 January 1945:* the Red Army enters the Auschwitz concentration camp and frees the surviving prisoners.

• *4-12 February 1945*: Yalta Conference with Stalin, Churchill and Roosevelt, held to plan the future world balance of power and the spheres of influence in Europe.

• *30 April 1945:* Hitler and Eva Braun commit suicide in the Berlin Chancellery bunker.

• *1 May 1945:* Magda and Joseph Goebbels commit suicide after killing their children.

• *5 May 1945:* the Mauthausen concentration camp is liberated.

• *23 May 1945:* Heinrich Himmler commits suicide.

• *20 November 1945:* the Nuremberg trial begins.

AN ADOLESCENT
IN ARTISTIC VIENNA
LEARNS TO HATE
THE WORLD

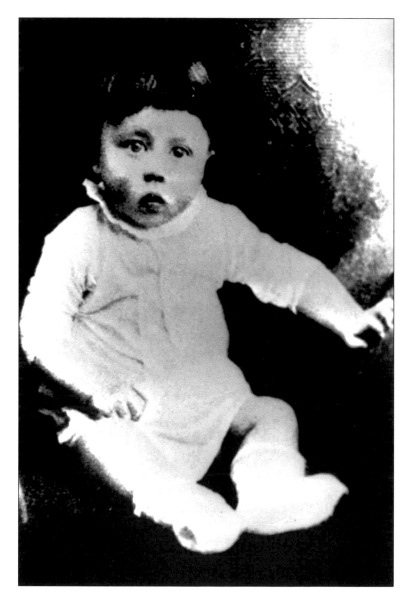

The 18-month old Hitler in his home in Braunau am Inn. He was born on April 20, 1889 to Klara Pölzl, who was then 28, and Alois Hiedler (his real family name), who was 52.

A dolf Hitler was born in Braunau am Inn on April 20, 1889, at 6:30 pm, in a room at the Gasthof zum Pommer, where the midwife had brought his mother Klara as soon as she went into labor. Klara, whose last name was Pölzl, was 28 years old, and her husband Alois – the baby's father – was 52. Braunau is a little border town in Austria, separated from Bavaria by the Inn River. Austria had lost its Italian provinces in the Italian Wars of Independence of 1859 and 1866, had been defeated by Prussia in 1870, and had been ruled for forty years by the Hapsburg Emperor Franz Joseph, who was destined to rule for another quarter century.

The boy's father and mother were both from Spital, in Waldviertel, a farming community in the northern part of the country near the Bohemian border, an area dotted with hills and woods. His father Alois, born in 1837, was the illegitimate son of the miller Johann Hiedler and the farmwoman Maria Anna Schicklgruber, who later married, thus officializing their relationship. Only in his old age did the miller acknowledge Alois, who was forty years old by this time, as his son. This would give rise to legends of all kinds, for example that Alois was born from his mother's relationship with a Jew, although such a person has never been identified and, most likely, never existed.

But why the surname Hitler rather than Hiedler? This was due to a mistake made by the parish priest of Döllersheim. During the official act of acknowledgement on the part of the old miller, the priest wrote "Hitler" in the parish birth registry – a clipped name that sounded like the crack of a whip or a war cry. For the Nazis, this circumstance would also be taken as a sign of fate.

Alois Hiedler was a withdrawn, strict man who worked as an official at the Braunau am Inn customs office from 1855 to 1895. His love life was far more turbulent: Klara Pölzl, his second cousin, was his third wife. He was a widower twice over, as one wife had died of heart disease and the other of tuberculosis. When Alois and Klara were married on January 7, 1895, she was five months pregnant. Their eldest son Gustav was born on May 17, and he was followed by Ida, Adolf, Edmund and, lastly, Paula in 1896. Gustav, Ida and Edmund died in childhood, leaving the couple with Adolf and Paula, who survived the future Führer. Adolf's half-brother Alois Jr. and his half-sister Angela – the children of Alois' second wife – also lived at home. The two also survived Adolf, and they were destined to become involved in dramatic and obscure future events. Angela had a daughter, Geli, who committed suicide following a stormy relationship with her uncle Adolf. Alois, who went to jail for in 1923 for bigamy, later opened a beer hall in Berlin and then emigrated to England, vanishing without a trace.

In 1895, Alois Hiedler retired at the age of 58. Four years later, he and his family moved to a house with a garden they bought in Leonding, near Linz. He received a decent pension and easily provided for his wife and his four remaining children: Alois, Angela, Adolf and Paula. He lived four more years, a period marked by bitter clashes with his 'singular' son, Adolf.

Their first quarrel occurred the year after the family moved to Leonding, when Adolf was about to finish elementary school. He attended the Benedictine school in Lambach, where he had distinguished himself for his participation in the monastery's religious life. He sang in the choir – he was the one who, on Christmas Day, would sing *Silent Night*, his favorite carol – and there was even talk of the possibility of his becoming a Catholic priest. But when the time came to make a decision about his studies following elementary school, an argument broke out with his father, who had always dreamed that his son would become a customs officer or at least a civil servant. "I want to become a painter! I want to become an artist," said the boy. "An artist? Over my dead body!" his father shouted, as Adolf later recalled in the first part of *Mein Kampf* (My Struggle).

Naturally, his father won the argument and at the age of eleven Adolf was enrolled at the *Realschule* or secondary school in Linz. He was a terrible student. His teacher Eduard Hümer gave the following description of Adolf during the Beer Hall Putsch trial: "Petulant, obstinate, arrogant. [He had] a terrible character. And he was also lazy. He would easily get carried away by enthusiasm that dissolved just as quickly. He would react with hostility to any observation or reprimand. At the same time, he demanded a sort of unconditional obedience from his schoolmates."

Hitler was to repay these opinions in the same coin. Discussing his teachers in *Mein Kampf*, he defined them as 'madmen' (in effect, two of them ended up in an insane asylum), spewing opinions such as, "Their sole purpose was to turn us into erudite apes. If a pupil demonstrated the least trace of originality, he was persecuted continuously." The only exception was Professor Leopold Pötsch, a German Nationalist sympathizer who gave the boy a book on the Franco-Prussian War and the victory at Sedan in 1870. It was Adolf's first history book. He would later say, "This teacher made history my favorite subject." He also commented, "When we listened to him we became afire with enthusiasm and, at times, we were moved even to tears. Perhaps unknowingly, he transformed me into a young revolutionary. Who could have studied German history under such a teacher without becoming an enemy of that state [Austria] whose ruling dynasty guided the destinies of the people so disastrously…. and did not, could not, have any love for us Germans?"

This was the moment when Pan-Germanism stirred the imagination of the boy from Braunau am Inn. "We took collections for the Sudmark and manifested our beliefs by wearing black, red and gold insignias. We greeted one another with 'Heil!' and instead of the Austrian anthem sang *Deutschland über Alles*, despite the warnings and punishment."

Hitler was thirteen when his father died of a heart attack in 1903. Without his pension, the widow had to struggle to provide for Adolf and Paula (their two half-siblings had found lowly jobs in the meantime). Two years later, Adolf left school, his mother sold the house in Leonding and the family moved to Linz. Between 1905 and 1908 – in Adolf Hitler's late teens, an age when, particularly in that period, a boy became a man – he did absolutely nothing that was either useful or positive. Though he no longer wanted to study, he refused to find a job. Thanks to his mother, who was willing to maintain him, he spent his days wandering through the streets of Linz in the company of his best friend, August Kubizek, who was eight months younger. One moment Adolf would go into raptures over his unexpressed love for the beautiful Stephanie – a girl he would see strolling along the country road but whom he never found the courage to approach – and the next moment would fantasize about his future as an artist, a dream he shared with August. His friend aspired to become a famous musician, and Adolf a great painter.

He would often spend his evenings at the opera with his friend, listening to Wagner. He spent the rest of his time loafing along the Danube or reading history books borrowed from mobile libraries. They were an odd couple, Adolf and August.

They wore the same clothes and donned broad-rimmed black hats. Many years later, long after the conclusion of the Second World War, eager historians would grasp at straws, citing Hitler's alleged homosexuality and exploiting ambiguous trade books such as *Adolf Hitler, mein Jugendfreund* (The Young Hitler I Knew), written by Kubizek in 1953.

It was in this period that Hitler first went to Vienna, the capital city. He was there, again thanks to the allowance he received from his mother, between May and June 1906. He was barely 17. Fascinated by the 18th-century buildings, the Opera House and the Ringstrasse, he decided that, when he turned eighteen, he would return to enroll at the Academy of Fine Arts.

September-October 1907 marked the first big disappointment of his life. He went to the Academy and took the entrance exam, but was turned down. His drawings (he had done several heads) were deemed "stiff and anonymous".

On December 21, 1907 – just four days before Christmas – came the second and more serious blow: the death of his mother Klara of breast cancer. Hitler shut himself inside the house in Linz for a month, weeping unabashedly. "I honored my father," he would later write in *Mein Kampf*, "but my mother I loved." In February 1908, he left Linz for good and went to Vienna with "a suitcase full of clothes and underwear". Nineteen years old, he was about to encounter five years of misery and unhappiness. The city of music, dance, the *Heurigen* – the typical Viennese wine bars – and gaiety did not captivate him. Year by year, he grew increasingly morose and would later refer to those five years as the saddest period of his life.

To get by, he used part of the government subsidy paid to underage orphans and part of the savings his mother had put aside. Kubizek, who was vainly attempting to be admitted to the conservatory, joined him a few weeks later. The two shared a shabby room they had rented on the second floor of a building on the Stumpergasse. The furniture consisted of two cots, a piano for August and a drawing table for Adolf. For entertainment, in the evening the two boys would go to the Opera House and the Burgtheater. During that period, Hitler composed a musical drama entitled *Wieland der Schmied* (Wieland the Blacksmith), which was never staged. In July of 1908, August returned to Linz to spend the summer with his parents, and Adolf was invited to Spital by his two aunts. That September he returned to Vienna full of hope, determined to make every attempt to enter the Academy of Fine Arts. But he did not even pass the selection process.

Scarred by this failure, Adolf left August and, alone, nursed his rage and hatred of the world, turning into a loner. Long-haired and with threadbare clothes, he took on odd jobs. Hitler did everything from shoveling snow to working as a porter at the train station and as a construction laborer. At first, he lived in a furnished room at Simon Denkgasse but later, unable to afford the rent any longer, he requested housing at the public dormitory near the railway station of Meidling, on the southern outskirts of Vienna. After receiving financial assistance from his half-sister Angela, who was working as a servant for a well-to-do family, he spent the next three years living in the men's hostel at 27 Meldmannstrasse. These three years were characterized by fights and run-ins with tramps, police reports filed against him, living like an animal and occasional work as a porter at Vienna's West Railroad Station. Every so often, his aunt, Johanna Pölzl, would give him some cash to tide him over, and when she died in March 1911, she left him a modest inheritance. This allowed him to abandon manual labor and devote his time to his passion for art. He painted postcards that his friend Reinhold Hanisch would sell to tourists in the local taverns and *Heurigen*. However, an argument broke out between the two men when Hitler accused

Hanisch of keeping most of the money. Adolf branched out on his own, painting pictures and then selling them. Most of his works depicted historical buildings and other architectural works.

Can the Viennese life of this young man – whose admission to the Academy of Fine Arts would have spared humanity one of history's greatest tragedies – truly have been so dismal? Yes, although there were lighter moments, glimmers of optimism and a dream or two. "Amidst all this," he was to write in *Mein Kampf*, "as was only natural, I served my love of architecture with ardent zeal. Along with music, it seemed to me the queen of the arts: under such circumstances, it was not 'work' but the greatest pleasure. I could read and draw well into the night, and never grow tired. I became more and more confident that my dream of a brilliant future would come true, even though it might require many years. I was firmly convinced that one day I would make a name for myself as an architect."

His last two years in Vienna were also decisive for his political and ideological education. He wrote in *Mein Kampf*: "At that time I read enormously and thoroughly…. In this way, in a few years' time I forged the foundations of knowledge from which I draw nourishment to this day…. In this period my eyes were opened to two menaces whose names I had previously scarcely known and whose terrible importance for the existence of the German people I certainly did not understand: Marxism and Jewry."

Eyewitnesses cite Hitler – legally of age by this time and no longer eligible for the state subsidy for orphans – as a man who did not smoke or drink, and who ate only sweets. Moreover, he literally devoured books and newspapers, and continuously discussed politics with explosions of verbal violence that made a profound impression on bystanders. His three topics were Jews, Marxists and the Hapsburgs.

In particular, he abhorred the workers who had joined the labor unions of the Social Democrat Party, preaching equality and solidarity for the working classes. In *Mein Kampf*, he noted: "Until then, my acquaintance with the Social Democratic Party was merely as a spectator at their meetings. Later I was asked to join the trade union…. Everything was disparaged: the nation, because it was held to be an invention of the 'capitalist' class (how often was I forced to listen to that one word!); the Fatherland, because it was considered an instrument in the hands of the bourgeoisie for the exploitation of the working masses; the authority of the law, because it was a means of oppressing the proletariat; religion, as a way of doping the people in order to exploit them afterwards; morality, as a badge of stupid and sheepish docility. There was nothing that they did not drag in the mud…. I remained silent at first, but it eventually became impossible."

Likewise, his hatred of Jews continued to grow. One day, he met 'a Jew' on one of the streets of Vienna. According to *Mein Kampf*: "He was wearing a black caftan and had long sidelocks. 'Can this be a German?' I thought". And yet, things had not started out this way. He continues in *Mein Kampf*: "It is difficult for me to say when the word 'Jew' first triggered negative thoughts in me. I do not recall this happening in my father's house. Few Jews lived in Linz. Over the centuries, their appearance had become European. I looked on them as Germans. I did not notice their diversity, with the exception of their religious confession. The fact that they had been persecuted because of their faith, as I thought at the time, made me angry over any offensive word against them. Then I went to Vienna. In those years, Vienna had approximately 200,000 Jews among a population of two million, and yet the sentiments of the anti-Semitic press of Vienna seemed unworthy of the culture of a great people. Given the fact that anti-Semitic newspapers were not among the best, I considered them the products of base envy."

Suddenly, however, as if by magic Hitler started to perceive things differently. "Wherever I went, all I saw were Jews. And the more I saw, the more they were distinguished from other human beings. The inner city in particular overflowed with a population that, in its external appearance alone, bore little resemblance to Germans.... I finally realized that they were active in all sectors. Was there any turpitude or any form of indecency, especially in cultural life, in which a Jew was not present? When one cut such an abscess, one would always discover, like a maggot in a putrescent body, a little Jew. They were everywhere: in the press, art, literature, the theater. Here was a pestilence, a moral pestilence that was infecting the public. Therefore, I carefully began to investigate the names of all the creators of these obscene byproducts of artistic life. Though my sensitivity rebelled, reason could not avoid drawing its logical conclusions. The fact that nine-tenths of all filthy literature, artistic banalities and theatrical nonsense could be attributed to these people, who represented not even one-hundredth of the population, could no longer be refuted.... Favorable theatrical reviews always praised the Jewish authors, while negative criticism was reserved exclusively for the Germans. Their constant polemical tone against William II revealed their method, as did their continuous praise of French culture. The vulgar contents of their short stories revealed their indecency and even in language one could start to hear the echo of a people other than the Germans."

Consequently, true hatred was stirred in young Hitler, hatred that was not religious but racial in scope, coupled with a sense of physical revulsion and frequent sexual overtones. He saw Jews everywhere. The capitalists and bankers who exploited the savings of the working class were Jews. Court advisors were Jews. The leading modernist figures in art and music (abstract art, twelve-tone music) were Jews. And above all, the Social Democrat union leaders who dehumanized workers were Jews. Thus, the combination of 'Marxists plus Jews' became entrenched in him, and would become the very foundation of the National Socialist ideology.

As he stated in *Mein Kampf:* "I finally realized that the Socialist press was controlled almost exclusively by Jews.... The publishers were also Jews. I began to collect as many socialist pamphlets as I could, to study the names of their authors: all Jews.... And I finally began to understand who the corrupters of my people were."

A sort of sexual obsession (in *Mein Kampf*, he recounted his nightmarish vision of "the seduction of hundreds of thousands of young women by repulsive bow-legged Jewish bastards") and the anti-Semitic policy backed by Vienna mayor Karl Lüger, head of the Christian Socialist Party – albeit on religious and economic grounds rather than racial ones – also helped spawn this hatred veined with folly. Hitler borrowed the 'social' idea from Lüger and the 'national' idea from Georg von Schönerer's Nationalists. And he merged the two concepts in the doctrine of National Socialism.

These premises led to his conviction that there was a "worldwide Jewish conspiracy to subdue the Aryan people". The means? Marxism, conceived by the Jews "to replace the aristocratic principle of nature (predominance of the strongest), the numerical mass that destroys human personality, race, nation".

As to his aversion for the Hapsburg Empire, this arose – in young Hitler's mind – because the monarchy had allowed Austria to become a "conglomeration of races, a mixture of Czechs, Poles, Hungarians, Ruthenians, Serbs and Croats, etc., from which there develops the fungus that thrives in all the crevices of humanity: Jews, always the Jews."

His disdain for the Hapsburgs was coupled with his scorn for representative democracy. Hitler attended several sessions of the Reichsrat, the Viennese Parliament, and commented, "The mediocre, the stupid, the cowardly triumphed there." Above all, however, he noted that the representatives of the German population, equivalent to 35% of the seats, were always in the minority.

Adolf Hitler left Vienna in the spring of 1913 to move to Munich, to what he now considered his true homeland, Germany: the 'Second Reich' founded by Otto von Bismarck on the stock of Prussia, which had crushed the Austro-Hungarian army at Sadowa in 1866. For a now-fanatical Pan-German like Hitler, there was no longer room in the capital city of that crumbling empire that, in just a few short decades, had lost northern Italy, granted the Hungarians equal rights and bilingualism, and borne the continuous revolts of Czechs, Moravians and Slovenians. The true German capital was no longer Vienna but Berlin.

In Munich, Hitler sublet a place from a tailor named Popp, in the Schleissheimerstrasse. For a living, he painted billboards, shop signs and postcards that he then sold at cafés and beer halls, where – even more so than in Vienna – he would vent his resentment and his revanchist spirit with endless political debates. In Munich, he read the books of two 'masters' of anti-Semitism, the Frenchman Joseph Arthur de Gobineau and the Englishman Houston Stewart Chamberlain, and he devoured all the works of Friedrich Nietzsche.

On June 28, 1914, the Archduke Francis Ferdinand, the heir to the Austrian throne, was assassinated in Sarajevo. Hitler rejoiced, later writing that he realized what the consequences were: not policing operations within the Austro-Hungarian Empire, but a struggle of the German nation for its very being and future. And he added, "For me and for every other German, the most memorable period of our existence was about to begin."

Hitler had undergone his physical at the military hospital in Salzburg, but was rejected as unfit for military service. Consequently, on August 3, 1914 – shortly after the outbreak of WWI – he sent a petition to volunteer in a Bavarian regiment. His petition was granted and his first post was as a dispatch runner for the First Company, 16th Bavarian Reserve Infantry.

A CORPORAL NAMED ADOLF HITLER: THE MILITARY CAREER OF THE FUTURE FÜHRER

The famous photograph of Hitler among the crowd in the Munich Odeonsplatz while applauding the declaration of war against Russia. He left for the front on October 21, 1914, when he was 25, as a private in an infantry regiment.

August 1, 1914: a now-famous photograph shows Adolf Hitler standing in the crowd gathered in Munich's Odeonsplatz, applauding as Germany's declaration of war against Russia is being read. The picture reveals an exultant Hitler, who is waving his arms and – perhaps for the first time in his life – has a smile on his face. By August 1, he had already prepared his letter to volunteer for the army, which he presented to military headquarters two days later. He couldn't wait. As he later wrote in *Mein Kampf*: "To me, those moments seem like my liberation from the oppressive feeling of impotence of my youth. Even now, I am not ashamed to state that, overwhelmed by wild enthusiasm, I knelt down and thanked fate for allowing me to live in such an era. A war for freedom had broken out, the likes of which the world had never seen."

What kind of a soldier was he? Perfect, according to the sources used by Nazi propaganda to describe the Fürher's role in WWI. Never a complaint about the cold, the humidity of the trenches, the orders for bayonet assaults. Never an irritated gesture towards his superiors. Never a request for a furlough. Never a complaint over the lack of women. However, recent studies have partly demolished the myth of Hitler as a heroic soldier. Assigned to the 16th Infantry Regiment – also referred to as the List Regiment after its commander – he met other volunteers, including Rudolf Hess and Sergeant Max Amann, who would later become his most loyal followers.

Hitler at the front in a battle dress uniform. During the battle of Ypres against the British he won his first medal of valor, the Ritterkreuz *or Iron Cross. He earned his second medal in 1918 for having captured 16 French soldiers.*

After basic training, he left for the front on October 21, 1914. He wrote in *Mein Kampf*: "For the first time in my life I saw the Rhine, as we journeyed along its calm banks to approach the enemy, in order to defend this German river against the greed of its traditional adversary. As the sunbeams broke through light morning mist and illuminated the monument of the Niederwald Statue, in a single voice the long military convoy broke into the strains of *Die Wacht am Rhein* [Watch on the Rhine] and I felt as if my heart would burst."

Their destination was Lille, where the Regiment joined the 6th Bavarian Division, assigned to the 6th Army led by the Crown Prince of Bavaria, Rupprecht Wittelsbach. Hitler's baptism by fire came with the First Battle of Ypres, fighting against the English. The engagement lasted four days and the Regiment was decimated: only 600 soldiers – including 30 officers – survived. Adolf Hitler was a headquarters dispatch runner (*Meldegänger*), which meant that he had to dash under enemy fire to carry dispatches from the Company to the Regiment and vice versa. He was awarded his first decoration for valor, the Iron Cross, Second Class. His second decoration, the Iron Cross, First Class, was awarded to him on August 4, 1918 for single-handedly taking sixteen French prisoners. Many years later, he recounted this story during an interview with journalist Sefton Delmer of the *Daily Express* (July 11, 1939): "I took sixteen Frenchmen by surprise in a bomb crater. I shouted to them '*Vous êtes prisonniers!*' and pretended to give orders to other German soldiers behind me, although no one was there. The bluff worked."

In 1915, Hitler was involved in the clashes at Tourcoing and Neuve Chapelle, also against the English, and the following year he fought in the Battle of the Somme. In Bapaume he was wounded in the leg on October 7, 1916, and returned to Germany for treatment and convalescence. He rejoined the Company in March 1917 – with the rank of corporal earned in battle – in time to fight

in the Battle of Arras and, during the summer, the Third Battle of
Ypres. He was then assigned a short period of rest.

There are numerous reports, provided by his comrades, of
Hitler's continuous tirades against Marxists and Jews, the former
for undermining army morale with their antimilitary stance, and
the latter for being "more powerful than our cannons because they
control the press and have production, finance and the state apparatus in their hands." *Mein Kampf* reveals his explosion of hatred
for draft-dodgers, the Reichstag ("which should have been dissolved
at bayonet point"), political parties, which should have been outlawed, and profiteers, who should have been shot. Here are some
significant passages: "I hated those verbose parliamentarians and,
had it been up to me, I would have turned them into a battalion
of [farm] hoers.... Moreover, following the early news of victory,
certain areas of the press started to water down the general enthusiasm.... We Germans were not to forget that the war was far from
our intentions, and so we were to have no hesitation in openly,
and courageously, declaring that we were ready for peace. Indeed,
instead of taking these rogues and stringing them up by the neck,
so that their aesthetic sensitivity would no longer be disturbed by
the joy of belonging to the fatherland, warnings began to be issued
against what was defined as excessive enthusiasm for victory.... One
did not understand that it [Marxism] was a doctrine that aimed at
the destruction of all mankind.... Marxism, whose ultimate goal is
the dissolution of all non-Semitic nations, was forced to realize, to
its great terror, that in the summer of 1914 the German working
class had escaped from its spell to put itself at the nation's disposal.
The Jewish goats were left alone and abandoned.... While the best
were dying in the trenches, on the internal front these filthy worms
should have been destroyed. Instead, His Majesty the Emperor
opened his arms to the scoundrels, allowing them to recover, and
to gain followers and credibility."

The soldier Adolf Hitler thus arrived at the idea that it was essential to create a political movement as the only practical way to escape from wishful thinking and furious yet inconclusive dreams. And he decided that if he survived the war, he would do everything in his power to offer the masses "an ideal that could take the place of the Marxist-Jewish one". In *Mein Kampf* he wrote, "I often spoke openly with my comrades of these things and it was then that I developed the idea of going into politics at the end of the war."

The List Regiment returned to the front line along the Aisne, spending the entire winter of 1917 and the spring of 1918 there. On October 14, 1918, south of Ypres the English attacked with gas, and Hitler was temporarily blinded. He was sent to the military hospital of Pasewalk and it was here that, on November 11, 1918, he heard the news of the Armistice and the end of the war. And it was during this war that he finally developed his concept of *Weltanschauung* or 'world view' (a word he loved to utter, perhaps because of its strong romantic assonance):

– inexorable hatred of Jews;
– disdain for the ideals of internationalism and pacifism;
– absolute nationalism;
– belief in the inequality among races and individuals;
– complete faith in war;
– the essential role of propaganda.

Hitler developed his belief in propaganda by making a comparison between the German press, which was essentially pacifist, and the British press, which showed no moral weakness and focused exclusively on victory, expressing no doubts about the nation's rationale.

To cite *Mein Kampf*: "The superiority of the English in knowing the spirit of the people is demonstrated by the fact that they have always been able to give their wars ideal goals. No man has ever given his life for economics. One dies for ideals, not business."

NSDAP:
FROM THE
BEER HALL PUTSCH
TO THE RISE TO POWER

itler experienced the dramatic events that marked Germany's defeat and the end of World War I from his room at the military hospital of Pasewalk. Day by day, he followed the rapid-fire events, avidly reading the newspapers that were delivered to the hospital café. On November 9, 1918 the Conservative deputy Gustav Stresemann, future Chancellor and recipient of the Nobel Peace Prize, proclaimed the 'Democratic Republic', in agreement with the Kaiser, who had abdicated and fled to the Netherlands. That same day, the Communist deputy Karl Liebknecht – inspired by Lenin – proclaimed the 'Soviet Republic'. In far-away Petrograd, the Bolshevik leader was convinced that he had 'option rights' on the fate of Germany, to which he indirectly owed his rise to power. On April 9, 1917, less than a month after the Czar's abdication, Lenin and thirty-one Bolshevik leaders took a special train from Zurich to Petrograd, escorted and funded by the Supreme Command of the Reichswehr (German Armed Forces). At the same time, Trotsky was traveling from the United States to Moscow on the Trans-Siberian Railroad. The 'betrayal' of the Czar and of Russia had been accomplished

A close-up of Hitler in a uniform of the SA (Sturmabteilung or storm troopers). On June 30, 1934 he ordered the massacre of the high-ranking SA officers, whom he suspected of having plotted to overthrow him.

with German marks and American dollars. Now, Lenin was using rubles to pay Karl Liebknecht, the man who could have redeemed Russia from the humiliating Treaty of Brest-Litovsk.

Hitler feverishly continued to read the first editions of the evening papers. November 10: the Reichstag appoints Friedrich Ebert head of state. November 11: the representatives of the Reichswehr Joint Chiefs of Staff sign the armistice with the Allied powers. This was the most humiliating news for a soldier who had fought so selflessly.

Hitler was released from the hospital on November 19. He was healed in body but feverish in spirit. Traveling catch as catch can, he arrived in Munich, his adopted city, and here he discovered what had occurred in the capital. On January 5, 1919 the sailors mutinied in Kiel and the Spartacists' revolt broke out in Berlin. Defense Minister Gustav Noske ordered what would go down in history as the 'week of blood'. The Reichswehr soldiers, who had returned from the front, joined forces with the national volunteers of the Freikorps, the Free Corps, to put down the revolt, and on January 16, they assassinated Karl Liebknecht and left-wing revolutionary Rosa Luxemburg.

One month later, on February 19, 1919, Hitler was appointed 'official trainer' or instructor of the 2nd Bavarian Infantry Regiment, a way of providing a salary to an unemployed soldier who had received several decorations. The man who had suggested Hitler's name to the Regiment headquarters was a captain whose face was disfigured by battle scars. Pudgy and ungainly, he was nevertheless tough as steel: Ernst Röhm. A few days later – again thanks to Röhm who, as staff officer, commanded the section responsible for monitoring political groups – Hitler was ordered to attend the meetings of the DAP (*Deutsche Arbeiter Partei*), the German Workers' Party founded in Munich on January 5 by journalist Karl Harrer and locksmith Anton Drexler. The 'official trainer' Adolf Hitler began to go to the rundown headquarters nightly, and ended up joining the party – membership card no. 7.

Top *Hitler's* Deutsche Arbeiter Partei *(German Workers Party) membership card, dated January 1, 1920. The party was founded by Anton Drexler the year before.*

Bottom *Hitler (the fourth from left in the first row, squatting) among the participants of the German Workers Party congress, held in Salzburg, Austria in 1920.*

However, the minds behind that little group of staunch anti-Communists were not its two founders, but engineer Gottfried Feder and journalist Dietrich Eckart. The latter soon became the mentor of the future Führer.

Eckart – a journalist, bohemian and intellectual – was 50 (he was born on March 23, 1868), twenty years older than Hitler. He had lived in poverty until the death of his father, who left him a small inheritance that he spent on travels and on supporting artists and musicians. He had translated and staged Ibsen's *Peer Gynt*. He eventually moved to Schwabing, the artists' district in Munich. Eckart and Hitler lived on the same street – Thierschstrasse – and they became inseparable. Eckart called Hitler "my Adolf", and Hitler referred to Eckart as "my north star". According to an encomiastic booklet written by Alfred Rosenberg years later, Eckart was contemptuous of women. At the age of 45, he married a wealthy widow, but the marriage was short-lived. When Hitler arrived in Munich, Eckart had just founded the weekly *Auf gut Deutsch* (The Good German). The publication discussed "the worldwide conspiracy of the Jews," praised "true Socialism, which differs enormously from Bolshevism," and voiced only the opinions of "pure-blooded Germans." This was music to Hitler's ears.

From their very first encounter, Eckart was completely infatuated with Hitler. He taught him polite manners, refined his language – which tended to be coarse, violent and vulgar – and helped him gain party leadership. And when Hitler, who by this time headed the DAP, transformed the party into the NSDAP (*Nationalsozialistische Deutsche Arbeiter Partei*, the National Socialist German Workers' Party), he remained his most loyal aide, keeping for himself only the leadership of the *Völkischer Beobachter* (People's Observer), the party organ. Nevertheless, it would be inappropriate to consider their rapport anything other than a simple friendship between two men. Bayreuth, with its Wagnerian music festival, became their 'soul place'. In 1923, wanted by the police following the Beer Hall Putsch, Eckart hid in Berchtesgaden, where he fell in love with a twenty-year-old girl. He died in this town only a few months later, after completing his last book, *Bolshevism from Moses to Lenin*. In *Mein Kampf*, Hitler would later refer to him as "the one who sacrificed his existence to stir our people."

On February 24, 1920, in his new role as 'head of propaganda and mass unrest', Hitler attended the DAP summit held at the Hofbräuhaus. With Hitler's contribution, the 25 points of the party were established during the meeting. A year had elapsed since his return to Munich and, in the meantime, Germany had been forced to sign the humiliating Treaty of Versailles on June 2, 1919. The treaty required Germany to pay the astonishing sum of 269 billion gold marks – 33 billion dollars – over the following 42 years as indemnity for 'war damages'. Moreover, the country was obliged to turn over 800 'war criminals', including the Kaiser's sons and Field Marshal Hindenburg (when General Hans von Seeckt, Commander in Chief of the new 'peace forces' that could not exceed 100,000 men, heard this request he swore, "They'll never get them"; independently, he also drew up a defense plan in the event of an Anglo-French attack).

Thus, it is not surprising that, at Hitler's specific request, the first point of the DAP program was a revision of the Treaty of Versailles. This was followed by concession of citizenship only to the *Volksgenossen* or people of pure German blood, condemnation of unearned income that was not generated by work, worker participation in company profits, social security and health benefits that were mandatory for everyone, reinstatement of the draft, great limitation of freedom of the press (only *Volksgenossen* could work as journalists), the condemnation of "degenerate art and literature" (abstract art, twelve-tone music and modern art in general), the fight against Bolshevism as it was considered the "instrument of international Jewry," farm reform with the possibility of expropriation without any compensation "for purposes of national utility," the death penalty for usury, free education for the brightest children, and so on, in a mixture of Socialism and Nationalism. In short, the foundation was laid for transforming the DAP into the NSDAP. This metamorphosis occurred when, following a paramilitary escalation triggered by the enrollment of hundreds of war veterans in the party, Adolf Hitler managed to sideline the party founders, relegating Drexler to the position of honorary chairman and getting himself elected acting chairman, with Max Amann, his sergeant during WWI trench warfare, appointed as his vice-chairman.

On August 1921, the first SA divisions (the 'Brownshirts') – initially *Sportabteilungen* (Sports Divisions) – made their appearance in the streets of Munich. However, they were soon followed by the *Sturmabteilungen* (Assault Divisions), organized from the very beginning by Captain Ernst Röhm. The first parade was held on August 3, with men wearing boots, brown uniforms, shirts with the sleeves rolled up and military berets who sang marching songs to the beat of the drums. And they had a rallying cry: 'violence and terror'. "In Marxism", noted Hitler, "ideology and brute force are brought together harmoniously. We will do better." And he went on to note: "Violence? It is exactly what the masses want. A demonstration of force provided by a parade of men in uniform not only serves as intimidation, it is also an attraction."

This marked the beginning of the spectacular meetings at the Hofbräuhaus and Zirkus Krone, with 6000 participants at a time. They started with Hitler's booming assemblies, followed by the brutality of the SA, who would follow and beat Communist protesters, in imitation of the Fascist Blackshirts in Italy.

At this point, it is important to note – in agreement with Joachim Fest, the leading German historian on Hitler and Nazism – that the theory of Hitler as a fanatical madman, a man possessed who hypnotized the masses, is simply too convenient and simplistic. And it is also historically ungrounded. Recalling Hitler's speeches to the crowds, the French ambassador to Berlin, André François-Poncet, wrote, "Like a medium, he would go into a trance: his face expressed a type of ecstasy." Otto Strasser, one of his earliest followers and later his mortal enemy, observed, "A man with a comical mustache is transformed into an archangel. Then the archangel flies away and Hitler returns, bathed in sweat and glassy-eyed."

Was Hitler under a demonic influence? It is an intriguing idea but an unlikely one, although in his book *Hitler Speaks*, Danzig governor Hermann Rauschning wrote, "He wakes up during the night, screaming convulsively. He sits on the edge of the bed, crying out for help. He trembles and screams things that are confused and incomprehensible. He gasps as if he were about to suffocate." (These details were given to Rauschning by a 'reliable source', although no one ever discovered who it was.) In reality, Hitler was an astute, calculating man who knew exactly how to gain approval speaking from a podium. He was certainly histrionic and an actor, but not a demon. Underlying his behavior was cold-blooded planning, and he never did anything to hide this. Quite the contrary: Lenin's coup during the October Revolution of 1917 taught him that it was possible to win power as long as one had a handful of men willing to do anything. "I openly confess that I learned a great deal from Marxism," he wrote in *Mein Kampf*. "But not from its tedious doctrine of social classes or the materialistic conception of history. Nonsense. I learned from the methods of Marxism. I simply had to adopt their methods of political struggle, develop them and take them to their extreme consequences." There is no need to recall what these methods were: violence, systematic lying and the vilification of his adversaries.

Hence we have harsh and coarse language, verbal and physical violence, sensational provocation such as red flags, trucks filled with armed thugs in military uniforms together with trucks carrying workers – also armed – with their left arms raised and their fists closed. The important thing, always and everywhere, was to gain press coverage, in keeping with the catchphrase: "Let them portray us as criminals. What counts is that they talk about us and continuously cover us."

As we have seen, most of the militants in the fledgling NSDAP came from the army ranks. They were soldiers forced to demobilize following Versailles, who now directed at the Left all the hatred they had formerly harbored against those who had won the war. And the Allied committees monitoring application of the Treaty of Versailles simply bolstered and aggravated this hatred of the revolutionary Left.

Mention was made above of the red flags that were waved in front of the Communists' noses as a provocation. Soon afterward a symbol appeared in the middle of the National Socialist flag: the swastika. Hitler himself was the one who designed it – black in the middle of a white circle – but the idea of adopting this symbol came from a dentist, Friedrich Kröhn, who had one in his family coat of arms. Hitler liked the swastika because he recalled that he had first seen it painted on the helmets of the mercenaries led by Wolfgang Kapp, whose attempted coup d'état in Berlin on March 13, 1919 ended in failure. Moreover, it was already used commonly by various Nationalist and anti-Semitic movements such as Thule Gesellschaft (Thule Society), of which his comrades Anton Drexler, Dietrich Eckart and Rudolf Hess were members. To be admitted to this society one had to declare that he had no Jewish ancestors and then swear an oath under the cross with the bent arms.

However, the swastika with the arms bent clockwise was known in India as an auspicious symbol, since the sun 'turns' from east to west, or from right to left. There was also a swastika that turned in the opposite direction, but Hitler paid no heed to this: he liked the swastika with its arms bent to the right, turning at 45 degrees. The

Tibetan lamas of the Bon sect, on the other hand, adopted the swastika oriented leftwards. And an SS battalion of a thousand Tibetan followers of that sect would battle to the last man in April 1945, in the last-ditch effort to defend Berlin.

Just as he copied the swastika from Tibet, from the Italian Fascists he copied the SA pennants, as well as the straight-armed salute, which became the *'Heilgrüss'* in Bavaria: the Roman greeting together with the cry *"heil!"*. Hitler directed everything, from protocol to parades. He personally oversaw the lineup of the assault divisions and their theatrical 'performance', the acoustics and ventilation of the halls, regardless of whether the meetings were held at the Hofbräuhaus, the Kindlkeller, the Zirkus Krone or the Burgerbräukeller. He was a veritable movie director. At least one-third of the available seats, beer halls or circus tents had to be occupied by loyal followers.

In the first service order he signed as the new chairman of the NSDAP on September 19, 1921, we find: "All party members are required to wear the cockade with the swastika. Jews who are appalled by this are to be punished at once." His oratory was violent, aggressive, overwhelming. He uttered every word angrily, his eyes ablaze, his head thrown back, his right arm rigid, and his left index finger pointing to the floor and then continuously moving up and down violently.

Each speech (he would give as many as four a night) was preceded and followed by thunderous military marches, but his words were even more thunderous than the drums. Here are two examples, taken from the newspapers of the period, n which he threatens the government and the Social Democratic Party, respectively: "When we come power, may God have mercy on you!" and "There is but one sentence for you traitors of the nation: the gallows." In each speech, he was obsessed with attacking Jews and the "traitors of November 1918" and with leveling accusations against the corrupt

West, the diktat of Versailles, 'longhairs' (left-wing young people who, then as now, wore their hair *à la garçonne*), 'Negro' music, "modern and degenerate" art and democracy ("Germany is dying of hunger because of democracy!"). And his speeches always ended with the announcement of "a powerful Reich that will range from Königsberg to Strasburg, from Hamburg to Vienna."

According to a 1921 police report, "The orator spoke for three hours before six or seven thousand people under the Krone circus tent. He said that everywhere one looks there are Jews. All of Germany is dominated by Jews. It is shameful that the working class allows itself to be exploited by Jews. Jews hold the money, they are part of the government and they traffic and trade on the black market. As the Jew fills his pockets, he sets workers against each other so that he will always be in control. We shall not cease our battle until the last Jew has been driven from the German Reich, even at the cost of a putsch. Then he railed against the press that wrote rubbish about the last meeting. Endless applause."

His rapport with the press was an odd one, polemical yet rather tolerant. In fact, the Munich journalists did not spare him harsh criticism. When the *Münchener Post* filled the first page with the headline "He Wants Chaos in Munich", he replied, "It's true! We want to drive the people to armed rebellion." And if the press wrote that he had dubious acquaintances, his response was, "Better a German thug than a French count." Lastly, his speeches never failed to refer to Christ, who had "castigated Jewish usurers and was crucified by them."

To be sure, the milieu in which Hitler moved and acted was unique and provided fertile grounds for his extremism. In the early 1920s Bavaria had become the hub of right-wing reaction, with over 300,000 activists mobilized by the various political movements, all of whom united to overturn the "republic of the Jews" that was ruling the country from Berlin. On March 14, 1920 Bavaria's regional government, headed by Social Democrat Johannes Hoffmann, was overthrown and replaced by a government led by Nationalist Gustav von Kahr, who enjoyed the full support of the Reichswehr and the Freikorps. These were the only true forces of the country. After the failure of the Kapp Putsch, they had reestablished order at the cost of terrible clashes, with dozens of victims and executions, in the industrial area of the Ruhr, in Saxony and in Thuringia, regions where the Communists had gathered a force of 50,000 armed men in order to prevent any other attempted coups d'état by the right wing.

The young Hitler was certainly the most notable figure in Munich's Nationalist hotbed. As early as 1919, Dietrich Eckart predicted the advent of a young, violent leader capable of communicating with the people. "There is no need for great intelligence: politics are the stupidest thing in the world," he wrote. When he met Hitler, he understood that the 'anointed one' had arrived. Eckart was the one who christened him *der Führer* or 'leader', and one of his songs, *Sturm, Sturm, Sturm,* was also the source of the party slogan *Deutschland, erwache!* (Germany, wake up!). Later, during a speech given in November 1922 just a few days after the Fascists' successful March on Rome, the head of the Bavarian SA, journalist Hermann Esser, called Hitler the German Mussolini.

The Führer's picturesque and variegated entourage included figures from all walks of life. People of indubitable prestige, such as flying ace Hermann Goering, who had been squadron commander in WWI with Manfred von Richthofen, worked alongside the likes of former war pilot Rudolf Hess, who was studying at the University of Munich by this time, Hitler's ex-sergeant Max Amann, the Führer's driver and bodyguard Emil Maurice, beer-hall bouncer Christian Weber, butcher's assistant Ulrich Graf, photographer Heinrich Hoffmann, the refined and cultured bohemian Ernst 'Putzi' Hanfstängl, the ambitious brothers Gregor and Otto

Strasser, and Captain Ernst Röhm, the only one who was allowed to use the familiar personal pronoun *du* when speaking with Hitler.

Another follower was Julius Streicher, the 'Hitler of Franconia', who was known for a particularly vulgar, sex-oriented type of anti-Semitism, which he used to fill the pages of his weekly *Der Stürmer*. There was nobleman Max Erwin von Scheubner-Richter, who secured secret funds for the party, a Baltic adventurer who was among those who perished during the Beer Hall Putsch. Another follower from the Baltic area who arrived in Munich during the Hitler era was Alfred Rosenberg, who would become the 'philosopher' of Nazism. A native of Riga, he fled during the Bolshevik revolution and more than willingly testified to its horrors and, above all, attested to the symbiosis between Communism and Judaism.

Such was the Bavarian 'court'. But in the summer of 1921, Hitler decided to establish a base in Berlin as well. As a result, he stayed in the capital for six weeks, where he met General Erich Ludendorff (the acknowledged hero of the Great War alongside Hindenburg), Walter Stennes, the ex-commander of the right-wing Freikorps organization, and other leading figures from the right-wing and conservative Nationalist current – all of whom he impressed as well. Nonetheless, he returned to Munich with the same hatred of city life that had distinguished his stay in Vienna. In that type of life – he wrote – and particularly in the lack of commitment among young people and in the nighttime customs, "I saw the systematic attempt to overturn the rules of hygiene of a race. The Jew turns night into day, he stages nightlife and is well aware that all this slowly destroys people physically and morally."

When he returned to Munich, he overturned the NSDAP structure, getting himself appointed chairman with plenary powers. The first serious clash with the left-wing opposition came on November 4, 1921 at the Hofbräuhaus, where 600 Communists scuffled with about 50 members of the SA. At first, the Nazis confronted their adversaries, hurling beer mugs, chairs and tables, exhorted by Hitler at the microphone. Then their revolvers replaced their insults. When the fracas was over, the room was filled with dead and wounded. There wasn't a single bystander who came through unscathed. Impassable, Hermann Esser – who was chairing the meeting – went to the microphone and said, "The meeting will continue: the Führer will now take the floor." From that day on, dozens of Communists asked to enroll in the NSDAP. All the police officers who had rushed to the scene and then filed complaints were dismissed by police chief Ernst Pöhner and by Wilhelm Frick, head of the political office.

By the end of 1921, 30% of the NSDAP members were office workers, 30% laborers and craftsmen, 25% either in the armed forces or students and professionals, and the remaining 15% were shopkeepers or owners of small businesses. They abhorred both Communism and captains of industry. Their watchwords were morality, cleanliness, precision, discipline, promptness and order. Hitler announced, "Only those who are ready to face death if necessary may volunteer for the SA."

In the meantime, the storm of inflation was brewing over Germany, and it would soon degenerate into the collapse of the mark. Uncontrolled price increases began in 1920 and skyrocketed over the next two years. In January 1922, one U.S. dollar cost 191 Papiermarks; by November 1923, it cost 4.2 billion. While the middle class lost its savings, the industrialists who produced export goods accumulated hard currency and paid miserable salaries. The government soon found itself unable to meet its war debts. French president Raymond Poincaré was indifferent to the situation, sending his troops to occupy the Ruhr district, which produced four-fifths of the coal and iron required by German industry. This was a drastic move, and while the Berlin government initially called for passive resistance, promoting a general strike that drove the French troops to violent repression, heavy industry understood that the time for temporizing was over. Industry tycoon Fritz Thyssen, industrialist Ugo Stinnes, steel king Emil Kirdorf, and the billionaire publisher Hugo Bruckmann poured money into the coffers of the NSDAP, the party that more than any other incited Germans to take up armed resistance against the French. In Nuremberg, the party promoted a 'patriotic day', the *Deutscher Tag* or German Day, on September 2, 1923 against Chancellor Stresemann, who had ordered the end of passive resistance in the Ruhr. Hitler was the undisputed star of the show with his fiery oratory ("Those who betray the German people must be punished with death! We want the gallows for the traitors of 1918!" he raged). On September 26 the Bavarian Parliament proclaimed a state of emergency and granted plenary powers to the monarchist governor Gustav von Kahr. Kahr represented a more moderate solution with respect to the incitement to civil war bandied about by Hitler and the *Deutscher Kampfbund*, the union of paramilitary formations composed of the *Reichsflagge* (Reich Flag), the *Vaterländische Vereine München* (Patriotic Leagues of Munich), the *Bund Oberland* (Oberland League) and the *Kampfverband Niederbayern* (Fighters' League of Lower Bavaria). The time was ripe for a coup d'état, the event that would go down in history as the Beer Hall Putsch.

It was the evening of November 8, 1923 and the announced anti-government manifestation had started at the Bürgerbräukeller. As Governor Kahr spoke, Hitler burst into the room, took over the podium, pulled out a pistol and fired two shots into the ceiling, proclaiming, "The national revolution has begun! Six hundred armed men are watching this room. No one move! The Bavarian governor is hereby deposed! The Reich government is deposed! A national army has been formed under the command of General Ludendorff. The army and police barracks have been occupied. Soldiers and policemen are marching with us under the sign of the swastika. Tomorrow we march on Berlin!"

Hitler then turned the microphone over to Goering and led Kahr, military district commander General Otto von Lossow and Bavarian police chief Colonel Hans von Seisser into a room. He tried to convince them to join the new provisional Reich government, pulling out his pistol and saying, "I have four bullets left, three for you and one for me." They hesitated. Ludendorff came into the room and persuaded them to accept the offer. The three returned to the podium. Hitler announced that the government had been formed and that he was its head. The crowed cheered. In the meantime, Röhm had occupied the Defense Ministry on the Ludwigstrasse, surrounding it with barbed wire and machine guns. But when Kahr, Lossow and Seisser were released by Hitler and left to return to their respective offices, they read the furious telegrams that had just arrived from Berlin, together with a message from the Crown Prince of Bavaria, Rupprecht von Wittelsbach, asking that they distance themselves from Hitler. The men conferred and decided to order the army to step in.

It was 11 a.m. on November 9, 1923 and the march through the streets of Munich had just begun. Miles and miles of armed SA men, led by Hitler and Ludendorff, left the Bürgerbräukeller to cross Ludwigsbrücke and Marienplatz, heading to Ludwigstrasse. When they reached the Feldherrnhalle, however, the Nazis were astonished to find a massive police cordon. At first, they proffered the Nazi salute, but when they realized that the attitude of the police was intractable, the SA men tried to push them away. The police opened fire and in just minutes, sixteen Nazis lay dead and dozens were wounded, including Hitler and Goering. Only Ludendorff continued to march straight ahead, undeterred, his eyes glassy and his jaw clenched, heedless of the bullets whistling past him. He was arrested. The march broke up as everyone took to their heels. Hitler fled in a car driven by his loyal follower Emil Maurice, but he was arrested later. Röhm and his men threw down their weapons and

raised their hands. No one had envisaged this kind of action by the police and consequently had not planned any countermeasures.

The trial of the Nazi leaders (except Goering, who had managed to escape to Austria) for high treason – a crime that theoretically called for the death penalty – was held before a court of moderate judges who were not leftist sympathizers. This had been arranged by Franz Gürtner, Justice Minister and a personal friend of Hitler. In the courtroom, Hitler stole the show, haranguing those present at each hearing, before dozens of international press correspondents. He proclaimed it was absolutely necessary to wipe out Communism, "Germany's ruin". As to the events in Munich, "I alone am responsible," he said, "and I fully accept my responsibility: I am not a traitor, but a German who loves his people."

Ludendorff was acquitted, the NSDAP was outlawed and Hitler was sentenced to five years in prison. However, after spending just nine months at the Landsberg fortress, surrounded and venerated by his 'court' – and enjoying workouts at the gym, drinking beer, reading books and spending the afternoon dictating *Mein Kampf* to his loyal follower Rudolf Hess – he was released on December 20, 1923.

While Hitler was in jail, the leadership of the party (which had had to change its name into NSFP, *Nationalsozialistische Freiheitspartei* or National-Socialist Freedom Party) was entrusted to Alfred Rosenberg and Gregor Strasser, under the formal presidency of Ludendorff. The party presented itself at the elections of May 4, 1924 with the initials NSFP, winning 2 million votes (or 6.6%) and 32 seats. This was no trifling figure, but the DNVP (*Deutsche Nationale Volkspartei* or the German National People's Party), which was financed by industrialist Alfred Hugenberg,

◄ *Adolf Hitler in his cell at the Landsberg prison after the failed Munich Beer Hall Putsch of November 9, 1923. He was released the following year on December 20. While in prison he dictated the first volume of his* Mein Kampf *to his loyal follower Rudolph Hess. He finished the book at the Obersalzberg or Eagle's Nest.*

continued to be the leading right-wing party. Without Hitler's guidance, the fledgling NSFP seemed destined to shrink rapidly. At the following elections on December 7, 1924, it did not exceed 3% of the votes, which amounted to only 14 deputies in the Reichstag.

Upon his return from Landsberg, Hitler quickly revamped the NSDAP officially. It was during this period that the President of the Republic, Friedrich Ebert, passed away. The election of the new president was slated for March 29, 1925. There was too little time to prepare adequately and as a result, Hitler's candidate, General Ludendorff, failed miserably, garnering only 200,000 votes. At the runoff election, Hitler channeled the Nazi votes to the center-right candidate, Field Marshal Hindenburg, who won over his rivals, the Social Democrat Wilhelm Marx and Communist Ernst Thälmann. Hitler was absolutely determined to make a comeback after the Beer Hall Putsch and the blow to his political image. His first move was to send feisty, capable Joseph Goebbels to Berlin as *Gauleiter* (party political secretary), to replace Gregor Strasser, considered too left-wing and even pro-Bolshevist. Goebbels had specific orders: he was to implement a policy of violence against the Communists. This was the beginning of the punitive missions against the various leagues of Communist fighters, while *Der Angriff* (The Assault), the newspaper that Goebbels had founded and directed in Berlin, roused the people. Thus, the financing from heavy industry that had stopped when the Putsch failed started to flow into the party treasury once again. Nothing can explain the new bond between Hitler and the leading industrialists better than this passage from a speech he gave to the Hamburg Industrialists' Association. "Only if we win will Marxism be destroyed. The word 'tolerance' is foreign to us. We shall have no peace until the last newspaper is destroyed, until the last organization has been dissolved, until the last educational center has been eliminated, until the last Marxist has been converted or exterminated."

But rising from the ashes was proving to be more difficult than expected. At the elections held on May 6, 1928, the Nazi votes dropped to 810,000 (or 2.6%) and the number of seats in Parliament went down to twelve. The elections dealt a tough blow to Hugenberg's Nationalists as well, and they lost thirty seats out of ninety. The economic crisis of 1929 arrived, bringing with it the dramatic devaluation of the mark. The entire country suddenly ground to a halt, including the left-wing Social Democrat Party, which was on the way to gaining an absolute majority. Hitler grasped the opportunity. Placing the blame for the crisis on the Left, which continued to eschew a national policy, Hitler convinced growing numbers of workers to desert the ranks of the SPD to join the NSDAP, whose members rose from 27,000 in 1925 (the lowest in its history) to 290,000 in 1930. Little by little, the working class changed its objectives, transferring its traditional hatred of 'masters' and targeting 'the French-Jewish plutocracies' that – according to Nazi propaganda – were responsible for the 'meltdown' of their savings and for the appalling increase in unemployment, which in 1930 had risen to 22.7% of the workforce (when Hitler came to power in 1933, 6 million people were jobless).

In the meantime, Alfred Hugenberg – utterly indifferent to what we would refer to today as a 'conflict of interest' – entered the field, taking over the presidency of the German National Party. A newspaper and cinema magnate, he virtually controlled all the most important instruments of propaganda and the means for shaping public opinion. And now he was no longer Hitler's rival but a precious ally, partly due to his general orientation, which had never been contrary to street violence in principle. Thanks to financing from heavy industry received through Hugenberg (as the billionaire Thyssen recounted after the war), the ranks of the SA Brownshirts rose to 400,000 regular armed members and they spread throughout the country. Little did it matter to the Führer that his alliance with the interests of the captains of industry caused a rift with the revolutionary wing led by Gregor and Otto Strasser, who in fact left the party. The NSDAP quickly converted its platform, abandoning projects for land reform and the confiscation of property from large landowners, thus gaining the allegiance of the agricultural world and the great Prussian landed estates.

On March 28, 1930 Hindenburg appointed Heinrich Brüning Chancellor. A member of the Catholic Center Party, Brüning did not have a majority at the Reichstag. He thus began to govern by presidential decrees that were not submitted to Parliament for approval, a dictatorial practice permitted by Article 48 of the Weimar Constitution. A few months later, on September 14, the

November 1930: Joseph Goebbels (the first person at left, with the swastika on his sleeve) and Hermann Goering (beside Goebbels) applaud Hitler during a meeting celebrating the success of their party at the elections (18.3% of the votes and 107 deputies elected).

Germans returned to the polls. The results showed that the Nazis had made enormous progress (6.4 million votes, or 18.3%, and 107 deputies). This made it the second most powerful party in the country after the Social Democrats (143 deputies), while the German Communist Party (KPD) won 77 seats, Hugenberg's Nationalists went from 73 to 41 seats and the Catholic People's Party dropped from 45 to 30.

Hitler continued to direct the party from his base in Munich. The time had not come yet for him to move to Berlin. On October 11, 1931, a summit meeting was called in Harzburg, uniting all the right-wing forces to launch a 'Manifesto against Bolshevism'. Attending the meeting were Hugenberg, Reichsbank president Hjalmar Schacht, and the heads of the Stahlhelm paramilitary organization and the Deutsche Volkspartei. Hitler was urged to participate and decided to go to Harzburg. The Manifesto demanded Brüning's resignation, the formation of a national government and rearmament. It was on this occasion that Thyssen joined the NSDAP.

Six months later, Hitler decided to challenge Hindenburg, presenting himself as a presidential candidate at the elections of April 10, 1932. Though Hindenburg was reconfirmed with 53% of the votes, Hitler's success was far from negligible (36.8%), whereas the Communist candidate Thälmann had to settle for 10.2%. Following Hindenburg's reelection, the day of reckoning between Hitler and Brüning arrived. The Chancellor, certain that he was backed by the head of state and basking in his success, drafted a decree with Defense Minister Gröner that called for the dissolution of the SA. The Reichswehr, which had embraced the Nazi cause by this time, was vehemently opposed to this, and General von Schleicher successfully demanded Gröner's resignation. Due also to the pressure placed on Hindenburg by the Junker circles, Brüning's resignation followed. The government crisis was settled with the nomination of Baron Franz von Papen to the Chancellorship on June 1, 1932. Papen, who was acceptable to Hindenburg, was a member of the Catholic Center, as well as a monarchist and a reactionary landowner. This meant he would guarantee the interests of aristocrats and capitalists but would also be a shield against the populism of Hitler, whom many of his own allies continued to consider too coarse and primitive. One of Papen's first political moves was to dissolve the regional Social-Democrat government of Prussia. The Left did not react at all, thus sealing its own fate. At the time, Karl Kautsky wrote: "It is fortunate for the German proletariat if the dreams of the Communists do not come true…. the Communists are the abettors of Fascism." In the eyes of Moscow's supporters across Europe, he became 'the renegade Kautsky'. This was the period of the ruinous ideological clash within left-wing ranks. Thälmann's Communists reacted to Kautsky's words by accusing Social Democracy and the SPD of 'Social-Fascism' ("Reformism is leftist only verbally; in deed it is Fascist."). In short, the most burning insult a Communist could hurl at a 'comrade' who deviated from the Moscow party line was to call him a Fascist. The March on Rome in 1922 was still an open wound for the Italian Communists. This abuse of words would continue for decades (in postwar Communist Berlin, a memorial was built to the victims of Fascism, not to the victims of Nazism) and still persists.

The Germans lived through the last six months of democracy with one election after the other, in which each party hoped to better its adversaries. With the ballot of July 31, 1932, the NSDAP became Germany's leading party with 230 deputies, followed by the SPD (133) and the Communists (89), while the election marked a partial defeat for the National and People's parties. Over 14 million Germans (37.4%) sided with Hitler. Goering was elected president of the Reichstag, and when he learned that Papen had expressed his intention of offering Hitler the post of vice-Chancellor, he publicly stated, "The word 'Vice' before the Führer's name is downright offensive."

There followed months of uncertainty for the government, constantly put to the test by the acts of violence that the SA unleashed in every town across the country. For example, five SA who had massacred a Communist worker were condemned to death. Papen commuted the sentence to life imprisonment, but Hitler sent each of them a telegram: "For us, your freedom is a matter of honor."

Following a motion of no confidence, Papen resigned and the Germans returned to the polls on November 6, 1932. Surprisingly, the Nazis lost 2 million votes, dropping to 33.1% and finding their seats in Parliament cut back to 196. It was also a partial defeat for the Social Democrats, whose representation was lowered from 133 to 121 deputies. Instead, there was an unexpected increase in the number of Communist deputies (100), People's Party deputies (70) and Nationalists (52).

Hitler's partial setback prompted Papen, who was reelected Chancellor, to draw up a dictatorial plan that envisaged the momentary suppression of parties and unions. However, he was forced to resign following another motion of no confidence, while the Junkers and high finance decided to play a decisive role by supporting a move to entrust the government to Hitler, presenting Hindenburg with an appeal signed by Thyssen, Krupp, Bosch, Schacht and other ship owners, bankers and steel industrialists.

Caught in the line of fire, the old field marshal chose the middle ground and on December 3, 1932, to everyone's surprise, he appointed General von Schleicher to the Chancellorship. The general fruitlessly tried to cut Hitler down to size, playing on his recent and partial electoral defeat – in vain. Repeatedly in the minority at the Reichstag, he resigned on January 28, 1933. Two days later, Hindenburg made Hitler his Chancellor, appointing Papen vice-Chancellor.

A GOVERNMENT OF ORDER OR A GOVERNMENT OF BANDITS?

As soon as he was appointed Chancellor, Hitler's first political objective was to reorganize the allies who had allowed him to achieve a majority in Parliament (from the Catholics of Monsignor Kaas to Hugenberg's Nationalists and Papen's Conservatives) and to remove from command any person – including Hindenburg's men – who were not blindly loyal to him. The plan he devised to achieve this goal entailed calling the Germans back to the polls, influencing the results of the umpteenth election through the powers of persuasion of the radio and press, and the money of the industrialists. To convince his allies not to block his plans, he reassured them that the Cabinet would not be touched. The sole purpose of the new vote – he lied – was the definitive defeat of the left-wing parties. And as soon as he obtained their approval, he implemented his plan in four moves.

The first one focused on guaranteeing the support of the Reichswehr. On February 2, 1933, during a meeting with the top brass of the Army and Navy, held at the home of General Kurt von Hammerstein, he laid his cards on the table and explicitly asked for the support of the Reichswehr, in return promising their rearmament and guaranteeing that the armed forces would be kept out of popular clashes and problems involving public order. The presence

◄ *Adolf Hitler, head of the National Socialist Party, the leading German party with 33.1% of the votes, is saluted by the Reichstag deputies after being named Chancellor by the President of the German Republic Paul von Hindenburg on January 30, 1933.*

of Werner von Blomberg at his side, as Defense Minister – he said – represented the best guarantee.

It was then time for the second move. On February 20, he called a secret meeting with a group of billionaires headed by Hjalmar Schacht, bringing together the leading names in heavy industry: Gustav Krupp, Karl Bosch, Georg von Schnitzler of the chemical cartel IG Farben, and steel king Albert Vögler, the owner of Vereinigte Stahlwerke (United Steelworks). "This will probably be the last election for the next hundred years," Goering sneered. The men at the meeting immediately gave Hitler three million marks.

Goering was also the kingpin of the third move. As Minister of the Interior of the Region of Prussia (which alone represented two-thirds of the country), he expressly ordered the police to avoid all confrontation with the SA, SS and Stahlhelm. At the same time, however, he also told them not to hesitate to open fire in case of attacks from what he defined "formations hostile to the State". On February 22 he created an auxiliary police corps of 40,000 effectives, all of whom came from the ranks of the SA, SS and Stahlhelm. These forces were immediately baptized the *Göringspolizei* or Goering's Police. Given these grounds, during the brief electoral campaign there were several violent clashes between the Nazis and the police on the one hand, and armed Communist formations on the other. On March 5, the date set for the election, 18 Nazis and 51 Communists were killed.

At this point, it was possible to set the fourth step in motion: a dramatic action to convince left-wing moderates to abandon the Communist Party once and for all. On the evening of February 27, 1933 the Reichstag was burned. The flames were already high and the enormous building was enveloped in a cloud of smoke when Goering, who was the president of Parliament, hastened to the scene. He was beside himself, shouting to the press, "This is a Communist crime perpetrated against the government!" Turning to Gestapo head Rudolf Diels as if to confirm his profound indignation and anger – though knowing full well that the command could not be carried out – he ordered Diels to "hang all the Communist deputies this very night." A few minutes later, inside the burning building the police captured Dutch Communist Marinus van der Lubbe with two cans of gasoline. A few days earlier, the Dutchman had been arrested at a café for boasting that he had set fire to public buildings and threatening that he would soon set fire to the Reichstag. However, he was only detained briefly and then released.

Given that the fire had broken out in many different points, it was immediately obvious that the catastrophe could not have been the work of just one person. It must have required the mobilization of a team of men perfectly familiar with the layout of the historic building. An underground passage led from Goering's residence to the interior of the Reichstag. At Nuremberg, General Franz Halder would later declare that, during the Führer's birthday dinner in 1942, he had personally heard Goering boast of organizing the fire, but Goering denied the allegation to his death and no one ever confirmed the general's testimony.

In addition to the Dutchman caught in the act, the police also arrested Ernst Torgler, leader of the KPD deputies, Bulgarian Communist leader Georgi Dimitrov (who would become the head of the Bulgarian government following World War II) and two of Dimitrov's men, namely Popov and Tanev, at their homes. The accusation: organizing the Reichstag fire on Stalin's orders. Following the trial in Leipzig, however, the four men were acquitted, and only van der Lubbe was sentenced to death and immediately decapitated. It was strongly suspected that the fire was a colossal provocation organized by the SA "services" who had infiltrated Communist ranks. This suspicion, which has never been proven, was fueled following the assassination of Karl Ernst, the head of the storm troopers in Berlin, during the operations carried out in the wake of the Night of the Long Knives.

The destruction of the Reichstag shook the world, but just 24 hours later, on February 28 Hitler convinced Hindenburg to sign a presidential decree abolishing the seven articles of the Constitution guaranteeing freedom of the press, freedom of assembly, the right to telephone and correspondence privacy, and the right of the inviolability of the home. This gave the police free rein to step in at will. Within a matter of hours, 4000 KPD officials (the lists had been ready for some time) were arrested, followed immediately by nearly all the KPD deputies and many SPD deputies, and they were imprisoned despite parliamentary immunity. All the left-wing newspapers were abolished, and Communist and Socialist assemblies were banned. The ballot was just three days away.

On March 3, an overwhelming majority of those eligible to vote went to the polls. Hitler received 17.3 million votes, equivalent to 44%. With 7.2 million votes, the Social Democrats were the second leading political power in the country. The Catholic Center gained 5.5 million. Though the KPD lost a million votes with respect to the previous ballot, it nevertheless received 4.8 million. Lastly, Hugenberg's Nationalists won 3.1 million votes. The 52 Nationalist deputies, combined with the 288 Nazis, would give the government a narrow majority of just 15 seats. This was not enough to allow Hitler to amend the Constitution so that Parliament could hand him full legislative powers for four years, because such an act required the approval of two-thirds of Parliament. How could he achieve his objective?

Joseph Goebbels, appointed Minister of Propaganda on March 13, had an idea: a spectacular inauguration of the legislature on March 21 (the anniversary of the inauguration of the Parliament of the Second Reich, established by Bismarck in 1871) at the garrison church in Potsdam, where Frederick the Great was buried. This was also the church where – as German children studied in school – Hindenburg had gone on his devout pilgrimage in 1866, when he was a young officer returning from the victorious Austro-Prussian War that had forged a unified Germany, the Second Reich (the First Reich was the Holy Roman Empire).

It was the sublimation of nationalist sentiment. The venerable Field Marshal August von Mackensen, a tall and solemn old man in a splendid uniform and a busby of the Death's Head Hussars on his head, was surrounded by a bevy of generals, field marshals and admirals. They stood alongside Hindenburg, who trembled with emotion as he moved through the crowd. In an inspired and solemn voice, Goebbels personally provided the radio commentary of the event, which he had conceived and organized down to the smallest detail. All of Germany, sitting spellbound by the radio, quivered with national pride.

Well aware that there is nothing like the rituals of monarchy to influence the collective subconscious – and despite the fact that none of them were monarchists – the Nazis wanted the *Kronprinz*, the Crown Prince, at the ceremony. Under his gaze, Hindenburg stopped to bow before the empty chair of the exiled Kaiser, William II, before giving a speech welcoming the new government. Hitler responded with humble yet fiery words: "Not the Kaiser, not the government, not the nation: no one wanted war! But today, thanks to your understanding, Herr Field Marshal, we are celebrating the union between the symbols of ancient grandeur and the new powers of Germany." Then he bowed deeply before the old president, as dozens of movie cameras whirred and the flashbulbs of hundreds of foreign correspondents went off.

Two days later – March 23 – the newly elected Reichstag met in the Kroll Opera House. The government presented a decree to grant full powers. Hitler gave a speech whose tone was intentionally moderate, but Otto Wels, the SPD deputy leader, was indignant because twelve of his party members (and all the Communist deputies) had been barred from the room by the police. Wels rose to speak, uttering a chilling reproach that ended with the words, "You can take away our freedom, but you will never take our honor." At this point, Hitler cast aside all pretense of fair play and jumped to his feet, livid with rage. "You're no longer needed!" he shouted. "Your death knell has tolled! Your votes no longer count. Germany is finally free!" His words were welcomed by an ovation that made the walls tremble. The law on plenary powers was approved with the majority required by the Constitution: 441 "ayes" and 84 "nays". Only the Social Democrats voted against the decree. When the results were read, the Nazi deputies rose to their feet, singing the SA anthem, the *Horst Wessel*: *"Die Fahne hoch / die Reihen fest geschlossen / SA marschiert...."* ("The flags are raised / our ranks are closed / the SA is marching...").

Now there were no more obstacles to the Nazis' conquest of the State. The *Länder*, or state governments, were abolished by replacing the various presidents of the regions with party-appointed governors (*Reichsstatthälter*). All regional councilmen who were Communists were jailed, all non-Nazi judges were fired, and the SPD was declared "subversive and an enemy of the State" and was disbanded. The center parties broke up of their own volition, including Hugenberg's *National Partei*, despite the fact that it was the party of the Army, the Junkers and heavy industry. On July 14, 1933 a special law proclaimed the NSDAP "Germany's sole political party" and anyone who founded or joined another political party faced a sentence of three years of hard labor. To appeal to the benevolence of the labor unions, Hitler made May 1 a national holiday – Labor Day – and arranged for the union leaders from all over Germany to be flown into Berlin, where a massive manifestation was held at Tempelhof Airport, culminating with an accommodating speech by the Führer ("All honor to labor and respect for the working class!").

The following day, the SA and SS burst into all union headquarters, confiscating property and arresting their officials, including the two federal presidents, Theodor Leipart and Peter Grassmann, despite the fact that just 24 hours before they had hastened to Berlin, with everyone else, to applaud Hitler. To those who asked him to step in, Robert Ley, Minister of Labor and the future head of the *Arbeitsfront* (Labor Front) responded, "They're better off in prison." Speaking over the radio, Ley tried to reassure workers: "I myself am the son of a worker and I am well aware of the exploitation to which you are subjected at the hands of capitalists. Not only will we respect you, but we will extend your rights."

From words to deeds: in the space of three weeks, collective contracts and the right to strike were abolished, and the ordinary magistracy was discharged from the task of settling disputes, which were instead handed over to party-appointed 'labor trustees'. Employers, defined by Ley as "the masters of the house," were given absolute authority in companies.

A series of laws had already been passed to exclude Jews from public office, professional roles and teaching positions, but April 1, 1933 was proclaimed as the day for boycotting Jewish shops. At this point, there was no longer a place for Jews in any company, with the exception of the lowliest tasks. The 'masters' applauded. As to the few who voiced their disagreement, party officials arrived at their businesses to take over the top executive positions. Some tried to fight this, but they ended up in a concentration camp and their companies were expropriated.

Franz von Papen was still the vice-Chancellor, but the men who truly counted were Goebbels (Culture and Propaganda), Walther Darré (Agriculture) and Hjalmar Schacht, who had just been appointed president of the Reichsbank (Central Bank) in place of Hans Luther, who was sent to Washington as Germany's ambassador. The 'Röhm case' was still up in the air.

SA head Ernst Röhm, the only Nazi official who addressed Hitler using the familiar personal pronoun *du*, had always been a left-winger since he first joined the party in Munich. And it was precisely this leaning, together with his well-known and admitted homosexual tendencies, that led to his expulsion from the national executive committee of the NSDAP in the summer of 1925. He thus moved to Bolivia, where he became a military consultant to the government and an army instructor. While there, in the fall of 1930 he received a letter from Hitler offering to readmit him to the upper party ranks as SA Chief of Staff. What made Hitler change his mind? As the years passed, the SA began to get the upper hand. In August 1930, Berlin SA commander Walter Stennes had refused to follow orders from Munich, claiming that his men's wages were too low, demanding a larger number of SA candidates to the Reichstag and threatening a putsch if his demands were not met. Hitler thus became the supreme commander of the SA, went to Berlin and granted the SA a raise. And then he called Röhm "back into service".

Soon after his return, Röhm took the situation in hand: Stennes was deposed without any consequences; there was total support for what was referred to as "Hitler's path to legality" (e.g. the conquest of power by democratic means); the SA was bolstered by bringing in such prestigious figures as August William of Prussia, the Kaiser's son, and Prince Philip of Hessen. Moreover, known homosexuals were placed in positions of command. For example, Edmund Heines, Röhm's lover during the 1920s, was made the head of the SA in Silesia, and Röhm demanded that the new commander of the SA in Berlin, Karl Ernst, be elected deputy (following his involvement in the Reichstag fire, Ernst would be eliminated by the SS as part of Hitler's showdown with Röhm). Ernst was already famous as the star of the Eldorado, a well-known gay rendezvous in Berlin, and his nickname was 'Frau Röhrbein' because of his relationship with Captain Paul Röhrbein, commander of the 1st SA Division of Berlin. The accusations of homosexuality spread through the opposition press, also following an investigation by *Rote Fahne* (Red

Flag, the Communist Party's official daily paper), and Goebbels was particularly anxious to get rid of Röhm. Nevertheless everyone – beginning with Hitler himself – agreed on Röhm's undisputed ability to command the colossal armed force that the SA had now become, which boasted 2.5 million armed men by this time.

Following the Nazi rise to power, the rapport between Hitler and Röhm – who continued to address each other by their first names and to manifest a sense of camaraderie and mutual affection – fell apart. Röhm took every opportunity to talk about a "second revolution" and comment that the time had come to "settle accounts with reactionaries" now that the dangerous Communists were gone (*Rotfront*, the Red Front, and *Reaktion* were the two historic enemies of Nazism, cited even in the official anthem of the SA). Hitler did not agree. In a speech to the SA on July 1, 1933, he noted, "There will be no second revolution: this would only lead to chaos." Thousands of men in uniform listened to him in astonishment. "We have six million unemployed to take care of," he added. "We need capitalists even if they are not Nazis." This basic contrast added to the evident rift concerning relations with the Armed Forces. Röhm wanted to transform the SA into a people's army that would take the place of the small and aristocratic Reichswehr, which was limited to 100,000 men led by reactionary Prussian generals. The Führer was diametrically opposed to this, and he had decided that the future Armed Forces, which would save the country, would be headed by the Generalität. The mortal battle between Hitler and Röhm had begun.

It was to last a year, oscillating between bitter conflict and rapprochement, such as Hitler's move on December 1, 1933, when he appointed Röhm "the Führer's substitute in the party." And he made another attempt in 1934, on New Year's Day, with his letter of thanks to Röhm and the SA, which was published with much fanfare in the *Völkischer Beobachter*. (People's Observer, the Nazi Party daily paper). But the idyll was short-lived. In the middle of February 1934, Röhm made a bold but fatal move, presenting a bill to the government that proposed the unification of the SS, SA, Stahlhelm and Reichswehr into a new popular army, the *Volksarmee*, which was to be under his command. The generals revolted, advancing their customary reservations over Röhm himself and his entourage of homosexuals. Hitler declared that he was totally opposed and the two men refused to budge from their respective positions. Röhm's anger boiled over into violent tirades against General von Blomberg during Cabinet meetings.

At the beginning of April 1934, since Hindenburg's health had declined in the meantime, Hitler wanted to guarantee that he would be his successor. During the spring maneuvers, he went aboard the cruiser *Deutschland*. In the presence of Defense Minister Blomberg, he explicitly asked the Commanders in Chief of the Army and Navy, respectively General Werner von Fritsch and Admiral Erich Raeder, to abandon Hindenburg's plan to bring the Kaiser back to the throne, and to support him as the Field Marshal's successor as President of the Republic. In exchange, Hitler guaranteed that the SA would be cut back dramatically. The commanders consented. That tacit agreement would go down in history as the Pact of the *Deutschland*. The tension between Hitler and Röhm climaxed following a meeting between the two in early June, which lasted for five hours. Hitler would later tell his entourage that during the meeting he sensed Röhm was planning to murder him. The Führer then ordered the storm troopers to go on leave for the entire month of July, during which time they were forbidden to wear uniforms or organize parades. Röhm left Berlin, but before his departure he invited his friend Adolf to a meeting with the SA commanders on June 30 at Wiessee, a well-known resort town on Lake Tegernsee, in northern Bavaria. Hitler thought this invitation was a trap and began to organize his countermove. But there was a brief interlude first.

On June 14, the Führer flew to Venice for his first meeting with

Benito Mussolini. He arrived wearing his wrinkled raincoat and a soft hat, to encounter the Duce of the Fascist Party. Mussolini strutted out wearing a sleek black uniform bedecked with galloons and medals, and he was surrounded by impeccably dressed officials and ministers. The encounter was humiliating for the German dictator. He returned to Berlin to find a veritable turn of events. On June 17, Vice-Chancellor Papen, spurred on and protected by the elderly but moribund Hindenburg, gave a speech at the University of Marburg in which he harshly criticized the excesses of the SA, railing against what he defined as "Nazi terror" and demanding that freedom of the press be restored. Goebbels did everything in his power to keep the event from being reported on the radio and in the papers, but Papen had sent copies of his speech to foreign correspondents and the world press gave the speech enormous play. The *Frankfurter Zeitung* broke its silence and published Papen's speech on the front page. Papen then had a row with Hitler, threatening that he would immediately inform the President that he had been boycotted, shouting that this was "intolerable for the Vice Chancellor!" Hitler immediately grasped the situation: he was running the serious risk that Hindenburg would proclaim martial law and entrust full powers to the Army. He hurried to Hindenburg's home in Neudeck, and his fears were confirmed. Hitler was received by Defense Minister Blomberg, who was generally obsequious and quite cordial but now addressed him coldly, aloofly informing him, "The Field Marshal has asked me to inform you that unless the storm troopers' tension and violence cease immediately, the President will proclaim martial law and will hand control of the State over to the Army." Hitler was then ushered into Hindenburg's study to hear the President confirm this ultimatum in a subdued but firm voice.

Back in Berlin, Hitler convoked Goering and Himmler, and together they decided to take rapid, ruthless action to prevent a putsch by Röhm, though it existed only in their imagination. They drew up lists of 'government enemies' to be eliminated physically. Himmler would go into action in Bavaria, Goering in Berlin. The Army was fully apprised of the move and on June 25, General von Fritsch suspended all leaves, confining the troops to the barracks in a state of alert.

At 2 a.m. on Saturday, June 30, 1934, Hitler flew to Munich. The *Nacht der langen Messer*, or Night of the Long Knives, had begun. When he landed at 4 a.m., he found the SS of the Führer's Guard Corps, clad in black, waiting for him. They were led by Sepp Dietrich, who had already received orders to arrest the SA leaders and execute them at the prison of Stadelheim. When the 'executioners' reached the esplanade in front of the Hotel Hanslbauern, in Wiessee, all the SA leaders were still fast asleep. No one was standing guard, an unthinkable blunder if these forces had indeed been organizing a putsch. Edmund Heines, SA Lieutenant General in Silesia, was sleeping with his young male lover. They were dragged from their bed and slaughtered in the courtyard like animals. Hitler burst into Röhm's room, but the sound of screeching brakes and slamming doors had already roused the SA leader. Hitler threw him a dressing gown and ordered, "Get dressed!" Then he instructed one of the SS officers to place his pistol on the nightstand of the only comrade who addressed him by his first name. But Röhm haughtily refused to commit suicide, shouting, "If I am to die, let Adolf be the one to kill me!" At this point, the two SS officers entered the room and, at point-blank range, they shot Röhm, still naked to the waist and – as a police officer present at the scene would later testify – "his eyes filled with contempt."

The Night of the Long Knives continued with the slaughter at the Bavarian prison of Stadelheim and hundreds of murders throughout Germany. In Berlin, Goering had 150 SS heads picked up at their homes and shot in the courtyard of the officers' school of Lichterfelde, the headquarters of the *Landespolizeigruppe General Goering*, which was already known as the *Göringspolizei*. Plainclothes

SS killed former Chancellor Kurt von Schleicher and his young wife in their villa on the outskirts of Berlin. The two had been married for just 18 months. Schleicher was suspected of being one of Röhm's accomplices in plotting the imaginary coup d'état. General Kurt von Bredow, a close collaborator of Schleicher, and the dissident former Nazi leader Gregor Strasser were also assassinated. Strasser's brother Otto, who fled from his house, and Vice-Chancellor Papen, who was undoubtedly alerted by the General Staff, managed to escape with their lives.

There followed a string of crimes that would make even the most hardened gangster blanch. Three of Papen's closest collaborators (and the authors of his defiant speech of June 17) were killed: Edgar Jung, Herbert von Bose and the head of Catholic Action, Erich Klausener. Nonetheless, this crime did not prevent Papen from accepting – just one month later – the post of ambassador to Vienna, where local Nazis had just murdered Chancellor Dollfuss, as we will see below. There were also murders due to mistaken identities. In Munich, in front of his wife and three children, a music critic who wrote for *Münchener Nachrichten* and had never been involved in politics was taken from his house, dragged into the street and murdered by four SS men. His only fault was that his family name Schmid, which had one "t" less than the local SA commander Willi Schmidt, whom another team of assassins had found and 'dispatched' in the meantime.

Hitler also ordered many personal vendettas. Of these, the most illustrious victim was Gustav von Kahr who, as President of the regional government of Bavaria, had put an end to the Beer Hall Putsch by failing to keep his word to the Führer. Though he had long retired from politics, he was taken from his house and hacked to death with a pickaxe in a marsh near Dachau. Father Bernhard Stempfle, a priest who knew too much about the suicide of Hitler's niece Geli Raubal, was also killed, and his body was found – with three bullets through the heart – in the forest of Harlaching.

How many were killed during the Night of the Long Knives? A thousand, according to the 1975 trial of Sepp Dietrich and the other SS survivors. Hitler cited 74 in his speech before the Reichstag on July 13, when he had to justify his actions before the world press, which had compared him to Al Capone: 74 people "executed", plus three suicides. In that speech, he said he had been forced take action to foil a plot by Röhm and Schleicher, who were "in agreement with a foreign power" (he was alluding to France, though he never actually named the country) to bring down the government. And he warned, "If two or three traitors plot with a foreigner statesman [and here he was alluding to French ambassador André François-Poncet, again, without naming names – author's note] and they keep me in the dark, I will have them shot, even if they discussed wine or antique coins during the meeting. Everyone must know," he concluded, "that whoever raises a hand against the State is destined to die."

General von Blomberg and Hindenburg himself hastened to give the Führer the total solidarity of the Armed Forces against the attacks of the foreign press. Only Field Marshall Georg von Mackensen and General Kurt von Hammerstein dared to protest, but strictly in reference to the murder of their colleagues, General von Schleicher and General von Bredow, refuting the accusations of "treason against the homeland" launched by Hitler against the two illustrious victims.

President Hindenburg died on August 2, 1934, at the age of 87. The time had come for the Reichswehr to enact the Pact of the *Deutschland*. The pact was respected. Even as the undertakers were dressing the Field Marshal's body, the following press release was issued: "Yesterday, August 1, the government approved the unification of the offices of Chancellor and President of the Republic under Adolf Hitler. As of today, he is also Supreme Commander of the Armed Forces. The government has also decided to abolish the title of President of the Republic. Adolf Hitler's new title is *Führer und Reichskanzler* (leader and Chancellor of the Reich) and all offi-

A moment of the National Socialist Party convention held in Nuremberg on September 4, 1934. The Führer, followed by leading party officials, goes up the stairs to the podium, where he will deliver one of his fiery speeches. The conventions were held every year until the outbreak of the war.

cers are required to swear an oath of allegiance to him." The oath: "I swear before God that I will render unconditional obedience to Adolf Hitler."

On August 19, a plebiscite for the government law decree was held: 95% of eligible voters went to the polls, and 90% of the voters (or 38 million German citizens) approved the constitutional measures that effectively abolished the election of the head of state by the people.

The *Parteitag*, the Nazi Party convention, was held in Nuremberg on September 4. In fanatic exultation, with tens of thousands of arms outstretched in the Nazi salute, Hitler announced, "For the next thousand years the form of the German nation has been established once and for all." The Third Reich – the 'thousand-year Reich' – was born.

CHAPTER 5

HITLER'S OPINIONS: PASSAGES FROM *MEIN KAMPF* AND *HITLER'S TABLE TALK*

For many years *Mein Kampf* was the best-selling book in Europe; millions of copies were sold in various countries, beginning with Germany, Italy and Spain. Then, at the end of WWII it was banned virtually all over the world, and reappeared a few decades after the fall of Nazism, except in Israel, of course, where it is and will always be unlawful to publish. The first section of the book (an avalanche of anti-Jewish hatred) was dictated by Hitler to his faithful follower Rudolf Hess in the Landsberg am Lech prison where they had been incarcerated after the unsuccessful Beer Hall Putsch of November 9, 1923. The second part was completed by Hitler himself in his Obersalzberg residence after leaving prison at the end of 1924.

Fundamental principles of the future Führer's thought were his implacable hatred of Communism and Judaism, and the absolute need to extend Germany's *Lebensraum* or 'living space' eastward. Hitler had proposed different titles for this work that were rather complicated and muddled, but the publisher, the Bavarian Max Amann, who had been an officer in WWI and was now one of Hitler's votaries, decided to adopt the concise

◄ Mein Kampf, *the Nazi 'gospel', publicized on large billboards in all the German cities on the occasion of the German Book Week. By late 1939, 5.2 million copies had been sold in Germany alone. The book enjoyed great success in Italy as well.*

title *Mein Kampf* (My Struggle). The book was first published in
Italy by Valentino Bompiani and came out on March 15, 1934
as *La mia battaglia* (My Battle), with a preface Hitler had written
expressly for the Italian edition. However, the first section of the
original work was not included in this edition and was published
only in 1970 by Pegaso Edizioni, Bologna, with the title *La mia
vita* (My Life).

The other indispensable source of Hitler's *Weltanschauung* or
world view is *Hitler's Table Talk*, published in English in 1953
and based on two original German versions with notes of Hitler's
statements taken by Henrich Heim, Henry Picker and Martin
Bormann and later collated and edited by Bormann. So what was
Hitler's worldview? Elementary, essential and unambiguous. One
need only leaf through the statements gathered together by the
Führer's devoted follower Henry Picker to see what he thought
about his allies and his enemies, how he envisioned the future
and his ideas concerning religion. What is most striking is his
outright admiration for the English, which is no less outspoken
that his hatred of the Jewish people. Russia was the world power
he hated most, although Stalin wanted to eliminate the Jews as
much as he did. Hitler even goes so far as to dream of colonizing
Russia "like Great Britain colonized India." As to Catholicism, he
was totally hostile: "Christianity is an invention of sick minds,"
he stated; and the fault certainly did not lie with Jesus, who
according to Hitler was not even a Jew but rather a descendant
of a Roman legionary. Another surprising aspect of these spon-
taneous conversations was the prediction he made of the future
of transportation: he foresaw trains speeding along at 124 mph
and three-lane highways – just as occurred a few decades after his
death. The following quotations were taken from *Mein Kampf*
and *Hitler's Table Talk*, preceded by the above-mentioned preface to the first Italian edition of *Mein Kampf*.

Hitler's preface to the 1934 Italian edition of Mein Kampf*:*

"The peoples who fight for sublime national ideas have vital strength and a rich future. Their destiny is within their grasp. Often their strengths, which create communities, are international values that are more beneficial for the coexistence of peoples than the 'immoral principles' of liberalism, which taint and poison the relationships among Nations. The mission of Fascism and National Socialism, which are intimately linked through their basic, common approach to a a worldview, is to indicate new paths to fruitful international collaboration. Understanding their most profound meaning, their essence, means rendering a great service to world peace and hence to the well-being of peoples."

Passages from An Accounting, *Volume One of* Mein Kampf (*Reynal & Hitchcock, New York 1941*)

Chapter 7: "While Jews were robbing the nation and taking possession of it, the hatred of the masses against the 'Prussians' increased.... I could see this as nothing other than a very able move by the Jews, who diverted attention from themselves and deflected it to others; and while the Bavarians and the Prussians were quarreling, the Jews were threatening the ground under their very feet. The Jews were organizing the revolution and smashed both Prussia and Bavaria in one stroke."

Chapter 8: ".... I began to understand the substance and aim of the work of the Jew Karl Marx. His *Das Kapital* became perfectly clear to me, as did the fight led by Socialism against national economics, which merely laid the groundwork for the hegemony of international finance and stock-exchange capital."

Chapter 10: "It is the specific duty of the State to intervene to supervise the daily teaching of the press and prevent every form of offence. It must closely watch all journalistic activity."

Chapter 10: "The function of the so-called democratic press was merely to dig the grave for the German people and Reich.... not to mention the Marxist press, for which lying is a vital necessity.... Its task is to break the backbone of the nation and its people, thus offering them as hogtied slaves of international finance and its Jewish masters."

Chapter 10: "The Jewish press will raise a tremendous cry if anyone tries to lay a hand on this vital instrument and tries to put an end to its scandalous activity by making it finally serve the State and wresting it from the enemies of the people or from foreigners. But I believe that such clamor will be less disturbing for us young people than it was for our fathers. Twelve-inch grenades hiss much more than a thousand Jewish hacks: so let them hiss."

Chapter 10: "The sin against the blood and the debasement of the race are the hereditary sin of this world and the end of humanity that is submitting to them."

Chapter 10: "The fight against syphilis calls for a war to the death against prostitution.... Prostitution is a disgrace to humanity...."

Chapter 10: "Marriage cannot be an end in itself, but must serve a far loftier end, the propagation and strengthening of the race."

Chapter 10: "All rights to personal freedom must come second to the sacred duty of maintaining the race."

Chapter 10: "It is not a matter of half-measures but of using a scalpel most decisively. For example, allowing incurable men to continue infecting the others who are healthy is a half-measure. This stems from an idea of humanitarianism that would ruin a hundred to save one. The fact that defective people must not bring defective offspring into the world stems from true reason and its concrete execution and it represents the most humane purposes of mankind.... The misfortune of a century will redeem millennia of history from indescribable suffering."

Chapter 10: "Disease of the body is merely the effect of diseased moral, social, and racial instincts."

Chapter 10: "The world is the property of healthy communities."

Chapter 10: "The Bolshevism of art is the only possible significant spiritual manifestation of Bolshevism itself. Anyone who doubts this should simply take a look at the art of the States ruled by Bolsheviks, and he will then understand, with disgust, the morbid, degenerate works.... generally known as Cubism and Dadaism."

Chapter 10: "The higher government authorities never understood the essential function of propaganda, nor did they understand that with the intelligent and incessant use of its techniques, one can present heaven to the people as if it were hell and make miserable life look like paradise. Only the Jew knew this and acted accordingly, but the German and his representatives did not have the slightest idea of this."

Chapter 11: "Those who see clearly into the Jewish world, the Jewish people, will see with equal clarity the sense and final aim of Marxism."

Chapter 11: "Pacifist humanitarianism will be an excellent concept when the superior race has conquered the whole world for itself, thus becoming lord and master of the earth."

Chapter 11: "In this world, whoever is not of good stock is chaff."

Chapter 11: "While Zionism wants to make the rest of the world believe that the national sentiment of the Jews will be satisfied by the establishment of a State in Palestine, the Jews are duping the poor Gentiles once again. They do not have even the slightest intention of creating a Jewish State in Palestine in order to live there, but aspire only to establishing a central organization, with sovereign rights that will release them from the control of other States. In short, a refuge and training ground for future swindlers."

Passages from The National Socialist Movement, *Volume Two of* Mein Kampf *(Reynal & Hitchcock, New York 1941)*

Chapter 1: "Marxism will march with democracy until it succeeds indirectly in securing for its criminal purposes the support of the sane national spiritual world it has sentenced to death. But if, by democratic means, Marxism should find its back to the wall…. it would unleash the crowbars and hammers of the incited proletarian masses…. which would teach the bourgeois world how foolish it is to imagine it can use Western democracy to oppose the Jewish conquest of the world."

Chapter 1: "…. Marxism systematically aims at putting the world in the hands of the Jews."

Chapter 11: "The Jew, the destroyer of civilization, offers the most striking contrast to the Aryan, the founder of civilization…. Where else is there a people who, over the past 2000 years, have changed so little in character and appearance? ….This population has never given anything to the civilization of men and has always taken from others. Though quick-minded, it has never become a creator of culture. The seeming sense of solidarity of the Jews is founded on the primitive herding instinct, which lasts the duration of a common danger…. If they were alone in the world, they would not hesitate to devour one another…. Since they do not have their own state, they aim to subjugate other states, organizing Marxist doctrine in two different fields: politics and unions. And they are successful in both, thanks to a 'superiority' over the Aryan: the lack of moral scruples."

Chapter 13: "The Jewish way of thinking is clear: the Bolshevization of Germany, which is the suppression of German national intellectuals and thus the exploitation of the German workforce by international Jewish finance."

Chapter 13: "Within the body of each nation, Jewry will always fight with those weapons that, given the mentality of those nations, appear most effective and likely to succeed. In our anguished national body, for its rise to power Jewry uses pacifist and internationalist ideologies. In France, it makes use of the well known and accurately assessed chauvinistic spirit. In England, it turns to economic viewpoints and world politics. In short, it always uses the main qualities that constitute the mentality of a nation. Only after Jewry has used these routes to achieve absolute influence as well as political and economic power does it reveal the true, profound intentions of its struggle. And it destroys States, reducing one after the other into a pile of ruins on which to establish the sovereignty of the Jewish Empire."

Chapter 13: "The fight that, perhaps unconsciously, Fascist Italy is waging against Jewry's three principal weapons is excellent proof that, though indirectly, the fangs of this venomous power can be broken. The prohibition of Freemasonry and secret societies, the suppression of the anti-national press and the demolition of Marxism will gradually allow the Fascist government to serve the interests of the Italian people more and more, without heeding the shrieks of the Jewish world hydra."

Chapter 15: "At the beginning or even during the war, if twelve or fifteen thousand of those Marxist Jews who were corrupting the people had died from poison gas, just as hundreds of thousands of our best Germans from all social classes and professions had to face it in the field, then millions of victims would not have perished in vain on the front. If twelve thousand of these Jewish scoundrels had been eliminated in time, this probably would have saved the lives of a million Germans who would have been of value for the future."

Passages from Hitler's Table Talk, 1941-1944. His Private Conversations. *Weidenfeld & Nicolson Ltd, London 1953.*

"[When we colonize the Russian territory,] the German colonist must live on handsome, spacious farms. The German authorities must have splendid buildings at their disposal, the governors must have palaces.... Around the city, for a radius of about 18 miles, there will be a belt of beautiful villages connected by the best roads. Outside this will be another world, in which we will allow the Russians to live as they see fit. The important thing is that we rule them. Should a revolution break out, all we need to do is drop some bombs on their cities and the whole thing will be over. Then, once a year, we will lead a troop of Khirgizes through the capital of the Reich so their imagination will be struck by the size and grandeur of our monuments. What India was for England, the territories of Russia will be for us."

"I won't live long enough to see how this situation evolves, but I am heartened by the thought that one day the German nation will see England and Germany united, marching together against America.... We shall have found the ally we need. The English are unrivaled in their impudence, but I admire them nonetheless. In this respect we still have a great deal to learn from them."

"The Russians do not live to an old age. They live to about fifty or sixty. Why should we vaccinate them? We should stand up to our lawyers and our doctors once and for all: no vaccinations, no soap.... But let them have all the alcohol and tobacco they want.... Blacks become dirty only when missionaries.... clothe them. In their natural state they are perfectly clean."

"If it hadn't been for the danger that Bolshevism would gain the upper hand in Europe, I would never have done anything to oppose the Spanish Revolution. The clergy would have been exterminated. If they were to rise to power at home, Europe would once again be plunged into the depths of the Dark Ages."

"If I were to choose between Cripps and Churchill, I would take Churchill a hundred times over.... an elderly man.... an inveterate smoker and heavy drinker, obviously arouses less fear than an ascetic Bolshevik like Cripps...."

"If we want to be objective about it, deep down Churchill is no more than an out-and-out braggart without any scruples, armed with indestructible pride and, even in his private life, incapable of acting like a gentleman.... One can only feel compassion for England, for a country that, in a war as decisive as this one, was unable to produce a man better than Churchill."

"With its attitude of humility, the Church has always wormed its way into positions of command, also winning its way into the heart of the German emperors, starting with Charlemagne. Its technique is the same one used by certain worldly women who initially use charm to win a man's trust. Then they tug on the reins little by little, lastly taking them firmly in hand, forcing the man to dance completely to their tune. Sometimes, with a little diplomacy these women can even persuade their husbands (just as the Catholic Church did with the German emperors) that they are the ones in charge, despite the fact that they have put a ring through their noses and lead them at will, as if they were oxen."

"Our Foreign Office has the specific task of finding out England's intentions today. The only way to achieve this is to flirt with Churchill's daughter, but the Foreign Minister and his diplomats in particular are not capable of organizing this kind of affair in time, although success might well save the lives of many German offices and soldiers."

"Behind Stalin is the Jewish plan of the dictatorship of the proletariat, a plan that entails the proletariat's elimination of the current systems of government and then the rise of an essentially Jewish minority to power, because the proletariat does not have the ability to rule.... When this war is over, Europe can breathe a sigh of relief. That day, I will have driven even the last Jew from Europe and the plant of eastern Communism will have been uprooted once and for all."

"When the war is over, I will strictly enforce respect of the principle whereby all cities must be cleansed until all the Jews have left, emigrating to Madagascar or to some other Jewish nation. The cities that fail to carry out this order will be destroyed one by one."

"Even Stalin, talking to Ribbentrop, did not hesitate to say that he is just waiting for the moment when a large enough intellectual class is formed in the USSR in order to get rid of the Jews, whom he still needs for executive offices."

"If Churchill is a jackal, Stalin is a tiger."

"The new railroad lines that will be needed to connect to the east and that will require major expansion of the current railway network must be built according to totally different criteria than the ones applied so far in the Reich's metropolitan territory.... The convoys set up for these lines must travel at an average speed of about 125 miles per hour, and obviously our rolling stock now in service cannot be used on the new lines. Larger cars must be built, better yet double-deckers, with the top one affording a good view."

"The fact that Churchill is a 'wretch' who among other things is more than willing to mix politics with his private interests as a capitalist is proven by the fact that he had his grandson sent as a correspondent on the expedition against Narvik, in order to guarantee the proceeds of that coverage. Against a calculating realist like Churchill, words are pointless. To make yourself understood, you must use only the clear language of deeds."

"It is my firm intention to connect all the conquered eastern territories by means of a network of highways radiating from Berlin up to the foot of the East wall. But the conventional width of 24.5 feet will not suffice for these highways. Instead I shall construct a road with three lanes, for a total width of 36 feet, in order to make possible a flow of faster continuous traffic...."

"For our own people we must broadcast the facts as well as extremely incisive comments on their significance. Good propaganda must be stimulating. Therefore, our newscasts must continue to use expressions such as 'Churchill the drunkard' and 'the criminal Roosevelt' on every possible occasion."

"It is good that, during the course of this war, millions of Germans can see and study Communism with their very own eyes in its Soviet homeland. Viewed in the light of day, Communism loses much of its ostensible allure. What happens with Communism is similar to what happens with women: those who wish to admire them must content themselves with observing them by candlelight after night has fallen, when men's vision is slightly clouded."

"If the Duce should die, this would be a terrible misfortune for Italy. As I strolled with him through the gardens of Villa Borghese, I had the opportunity to compare his profile with that of the Roman busts, and I understood that he was one of the Caesars. Mussolini is indubitably the heir of one of the great men of that era."

"The Duce is experiencing difficulty because his army supports the king, because the International [association] of priests is based in Rome, and because the State, contrary to the people, is only half Fascist."

"I understand how one could go into raptures over Mohammed's paradise, but the insipid heaven of Christians! In life you listened to the music of Richard Wagner. After death, there will be nothing more than hallelujahs, the waving of branches, suckling babies and grizzled old men…. Christianity is an invention of sick minds…. A black man, with his taboos, is overwhelmingly superior to the human being who seriously believes in transubstantiation."

"Jesus was certainly not a Jew. The Jews would not have handed over one of their own to Roman justice. They would have condemned him themselves. It is likely that numerous descendants of the Roman legionaries, mostly Gauls, lived in Galilee, and Jesus must have been one of them. Instead, one cannot exclude the possibility that his mother was Jewish.

"Jesus fought against the materialism that was corrupting his era, and thus against the Jews.

"Paul of Tarsus, who was initially one of the Christians' most persistent adversaries, suddenly perceived the possibility of using – intelligently and for other purposes – an idea that exerted similar power of seduction. He realized that the shrewd exploitation of an idea of this kind would earn him greater power among non-Jews than the promise of material rewards made to the Jews themselves. It was then that the man who would become St. Paul distorted the Christian idea with diabolical subtlety. He turned this idea, which contained a declaration of war against the golden calf, the selfishness and the materialism of the Jews, into the cry of alliance of slaves of all kinds against the elite, against masters, against rulers. The religion crafted by Paul of Tarsus, which would henceforth be called Christianity, and Communism are one and the same."

Members of the Hitler Youth during a reading from Mein Kampf. *The obsessive theme of Hitler's book is the need for an all-out war against Communism and above all against Judaism, "whose aim," he writes, "is the Bolshevization of Germany."*

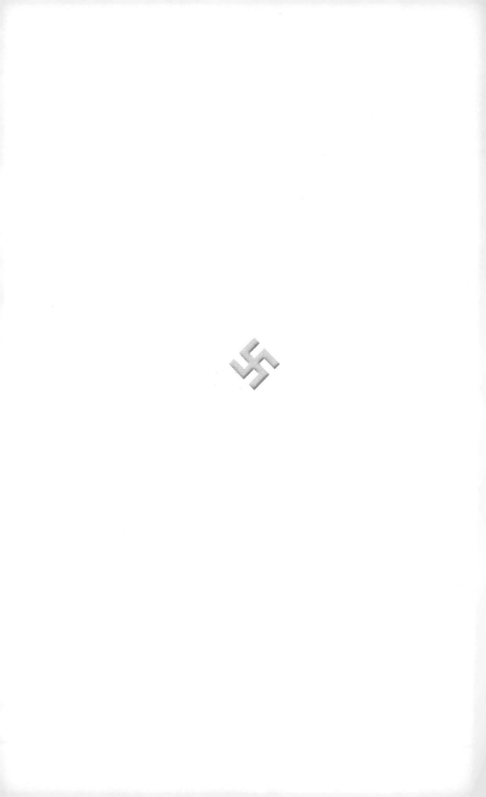

Chapter 6

THE 'NEW ORDER' TRANSFORMS GERMANY

On the evening of May 10, 1933 a procession of thousands of students carrying flaming torches moved along Unter den Linden to the square in front of the University of Berlin. In the square, they threw their torches on a pile of 20,000 books. This was the beginning of the "book burnings", a symbolic event studied and organized by the new Minister of Propaganda, Joseph Goebbels. Most of the greatest writers – Germans and foreigners alike – who were judged 'subversive' or capable of what Goebbels referred to as "undermining German thought" were outlawed in the new Germany. Hundreds of bonfires were lit to burn the works of German novelists, philosophers, scientists and politicians, such as Thomas Mann, Albert Einstein, Arnold and Stefan Zweig, Erich Maria Remarque, Walther Rathenau and Hugo Preuss, the principal drafter of the constitution of the Weimar Republic. Many of these writers were Jewish. The foreigners whose names ended up on the list – and whose works were burned – included scientists such as Sigmund Freud as well as literary giants like Jack London, André Gide, Marcel Proust, Arthur Schnitzler, Havelock Ellis, H.G. Wells and Emile Zola. "These flames," said

◄ *May 10, 1933: book burning in the square in front of the University of Berlin. From that day on, tens of thousands of books – written by famous authors, thinkers and philosophers, both German and foreign, and considered subversive by Joseph Goebbels' 'cultural consultants' – were burned.*

Goebbels during the first book burning, "illuminate the end of the old world and the beginning of the new order." The publication and sale of books by 'listed' authors were banned throughout the country and publishers were urged to print and circulate texts praising Nazism. The Nazification of culture culminated in the creation of the Reich Chamber of Culture on September 22, 1933. Headed by Goebbels, it was divided into seven 'departments' dealing with different sectors: fine arts, music, literature, theater, radio, cinema and the press. Each department was headed by one of Goebbels' loyal followers. According to William Shirer, the leading historian of Nazism, the unsuccessful playwright Hans Johst, who headed the Theater Department, was the one who uttered a phrase that became famous: "When I hear the word 'culture', I instinctively reach for my gun." But perhaps Johst had heard this in turn from Röhm, who according to numerous witnesses would encourage his storm troopers with the words, "When you hear the word 'culture', take out your revolver!" The fact is that, from then on, every book, every play, every art exhibit had to receive the *nihil obstat* or authorization of the Propaganda Ministry. And after setting the rules about which books could be published, the ministry's next step was to ban the performance of any play, opera or symphony written by Jews; thus, no more Mendelssohn, no more Hindemith.

Some composers and conductors submitted to this policy. However, the most astonishing example of this capitulation was Gerhart Hauptmann, the playwright who, as an ardent Socialist, had been worshipped in Weimar. Declaring himself a committed Nazi, he effectively became Goebbels' testimonial. Following the war, his works were banned in the US but, after atoning for his faith in the Third Reich, he was welcomed to East Berlin as a hero of Socialism.

In the figurative arts, the Nazification of culture proceeded under the direct supervision of the Führer, an 'expert' in the field.

The first thing he did was to ban experiences like the Bauhaus, Impressionism and Cubism, citing the motto he had coined: "The works of art that people cannot understand but that require an excessive number of explanations must no longer be brought to the attention of German citizens." Thus, no less than 6500 'decadent' works – by masters such as Grosz, Van Gogh, Picasso, Gauguin, Matisse and Chagall – were taken down from museum walls and replaced with Nazi artwork.

Above all, however, it was by dominating the press, radio and film industry that Nazism penetrated into the minds, souls and hearts of the Germans. Every morning, a meeting was held at the Propaganda Ministry, involving the editors in chief of the dailies published in the capital city and the correspondents of the leading provincial papers. Those attending the meeting were given a hand-out indicating not only which news was to be published or omitted, but also the contents of the headlines, the layout of the articles and the photographs to be used. This policy was modeled after the example set in Fascist Italy, where Mussolini had entrusted this task to his son-in-law Galeazzo Ciano. In Germany, however, it was conducted with 'German rigor' – in other words, to the extreme. The 'poor' papers that did not have a Berlin office received these handouts by telegraph (and later, by teletype). With the law passed on October 4, 1933, journalism became a 'public profession': journalists had to be German and of Aryan stock, and they could not marry Jewish women. The papers with a long Jewish tradition were abolished, starting with the *Vossische Zeitung* published by Ullstein (it was founded in 1704 and Frederick the Great had also contributed to it), and the *Berliner Tageblatt* published by Lackman-Mosse. The *Frankfurter Zeitung* and *Deutsche Allgemeine Zeitung*, the daily newspapers with the largest circulation, were also owned by Jews but kept on publishing. First, these owners were removed and the papers were absorbed by Eher Verlag, the Nazi publishing

Joseph Goebbels, the Minister of Propaganda, attending a military parade next to his idol, to whom he would sacrifice his life and that of his wife Magda Quandt and their six children, whose names all began with the letter letter 'H'. At the time this photo was shot, Goebbels was 38 and Hitler 46.

house headed by Hitler's former sergeant and loyal follower Max Amann. Because they were world-famous, the two papers had to be maintained, but they were transformed into propaganda tools. This was effected by their being covered by the 'fig leaf' of two London-based correspondents, Rudolf Kircher and Karl Silex, who were professed liberals obviously willing to serve the new master. As long as Goebbels was the one to claim that Hitler was a good-hearted and gentle pacifist, no one believed it. But it was a different matter if those making this statement were notables like Kircher and Silex. Following the war, this lesson would be assimilated perfectly by European capitalists, Italians and Germans in particular, who preferred to entrust their media of communication to journalists with a Marxist background.

The Radio and Film Departments were personally overseen by Goebbels, who had immediately grasped that "radio is the most effective means of propaganda of our age." Paul Joseph Goebbels was born to a working class family in Rheydt (Rhineland) on October 29, 1897. Raised as a Catholic, he studied the classics and graduated from the University of Heidelberg in 1921 with a degree in philosophy. He hoped to become a reporter with the *Berliner Tageblatt*, but after working for them occasionally, he was finally turned down. Surgery performed on his left femur when he was a boy (and not a cloven foot, as was later written by historians and journalists in an attempt to demonize him even further) left him with a noticeable limp. This condition led to his being rejected for military service in WWI, a misfortune that made him bitter and resentful. Though physically unattractive, Goebbels was always surrounded by beautiful women even before becoming Propaganda Minister and *deus ex machina* of the movie industry, roles that would lead to a string of relationships with actresses, dancers and pinup girls. Nevertheless, the only woman he truly loved, even more than life itself, was his wife, Magda Quandt who, by a strange twist of fate, was so deeply in love with Adolf Hitler – an unrequited love – that she was willing to marry Goebbels and bear him six children simply to be able to work at the side of her idol, the Führer.

Goebbels joined the NSDAP in 1924 after hearing Hitler speak in Munich. Despite his undisputed intelligence, however, he did not emerge immediately and was 'discovered' by Gregor Strasser only three years later. It was Strasser who decided to use him, hiring him as his secretary in place of Heinrich Himmler who, following the failed Beer Hall Putsch in 1923, decided to become a sheep farmer. Strasser immediately recognized the cultural difference between the two men. Goebbels was as brilliant and educated (well-versed in Greek, Latin, history, philosophy and literature) as Himmler was rigid and obtuse. And Goebbels was both an enthralling speaker and a brilliant writer, two talents that are rarely found in one person. Moreover, Strasser and Goebbels shared a belief in the Left and in the working class. Like his 'principal', he considered himself "a real Socialist" and if forced to choose, he had no doubts whatsoever: "Better Bolshevism than capitalism," he wrote in his diary on October 23, 1925.

During his early years in politics, his vigorous left-wing leanings had led to clashes with Hitler himself, driving him to embrace causes like the SPD and KPD demand to expropriate the lands and castles of the royal house, the Wittelsbach family and all the former noble families deposed following the Weimar Republic. During a stormy meeting of the NSDAP leaders held in Hanover, during which Hitler tried to impress on those present that much of the party's funding came from none other than the nobles of the past, Goebbels had even demanded that "the petty bourgeois Adolf Hitler" be expelled from the party. Going against his own instinct, but in all likelihood due to the mediation of Magda Quandt, the future Führer tried to smooth the rough edges of that brash young man, inviting him to hold a series of conferences in Munich.

The first of these conferences was held at the legendary Bürgerbräukeller. Goebbels arrived in the car that Hitler had sent to the station to receive his guest. He spoke for two and a half hours, to the thunderous applause of thousands of Nazis. When he finished, Hitler embraced him, and this was all it took to win Goebbels over completely. Following the Hanover meeting, he had noted in his diary: "What sort of Hitler is this? Italy and England our natural allies? Horrible! We must annihilate Russia? Horrible! The issue of the private property of the nobility must not even be mentioned? Horrible!" Yet just two months later, during his conferences in Munich, he wrote in his diary (April 13, 1926): "Hitler spoke for three hours. Marvelous! Italy and England our allies. Russia wants to devour us. I love him! I bow to the superior man, to the political genius." Goebbels spent that summer in the leader's villa at Obersalzberg and also had a sensational rift with Strasser. Hitler appointed him *Gauleiter* (district leader) of Berlin, the quintessential 'Red' city, entrusting him with the task of converting it to Nazism.

As was the case with every other sector of cultural life, the Nazification of schools was swift and totalitarian. This task was given to Bernhard Rust, SA *Obergruppenführer* and former district leader of Hanover, whom Hitler appointed Minister of Science, Education and Popular Culture (like every reformer, the Führer was careful to alter the traditional responsibilities of the ministries). Rust's academic credentials? He was an elementary school teacher. For that matter, Benito Mussolini, the Duce of much-envied Fascist Italy, was an ordinary elementary school teacher. Rust wasted no time. Textbooks were quickly rewritten by party journalists, and professors were ordered to memorize *Mein Kampf*, in which Hitler lambastes teachers. Everyone had to attend special courses on Nazi doctrine, join the National Teachers' League and swear loyalty and obedience to Adolf Hitler (in Italy, Mussolini had settled for an oath of allegiance to Fascism). Jews were immediately expelled from teaching positions at high schools and universities, despite the fact that between 1905 and 1931 no less than ten German Jews had won the Nobel Prize in sciences. One of the men who was expelled was Albert Einstein who, along with Karl Jaspers, Theodor Litt, Karl Barth, the Mann family, Sigmund Freud and dozens of other luminaries, found refuge abroad. This brain drain was also one of the reasons why Germany lost the atom bomb race ten years later.

The next step was to win over German youth. Hitler gave this assignment to the young Baldur von Schirach, appointing him Youth Leader of the Reich in June 1933. When he had joined the party in 1925, Schirach was not even 18 years old. Of Austrian origin like the Führer, he had American forebears, including two who had signed the Declaration of Independence. He carried out his task with great organizational ability, likewise using Fascist Italy – where young people were divided into the *Figli della Lupa*, *Balilla*, *Avanguardisti* and *Giovani Fascisti* youth movements – as his model.

All children between the ages of 6 and 18 were enrolled in the *Hitlerjugend* or Hitler Youth. When they turned 10 they had to participate in ceremonies in which they swore an oath: "I swear to devote all my energies to the savior of our country, Adolf Hitler. I am willing to give my life for him, so help me God." At the age of 14, everyone – both boys and girls (the latter were united in the *Bund Deutscher Mädel*, or League of German Girls, and had to wear a white blouse, dark skirt and climbing boots) – had to undergo courses in paramilitary training, sports and ideology. When they turned 18, the boys could choose to serve in the Army or the RAD (*Reicharbeitsdienst*, Reich Labor Service). The eighteen-year-olds leaving the *Hitlerjugend* who did not join the military were the ones who provided the enormous workforce that in just three years – from 1935 to 1938 – allowed Germany to build its spectacular network of nearly 2000 miles of four-lane highways, which not only lent enormous impetus to the burgeoning automotive industry but would turn out to be an instrument for swift military intervention, as would be demonstrated in September 1939.

The institutes established by the Fascist regime in Italy were also mimicked with the establishment of the *Arbeitsfront*, the Labor Front, created through the law enacted on October 24, 1934. The man appointed to head the Front was Minister Robert Ley, who was privately referred to by billionaire Thyssen as "that stuttering drunkard." In Italy, within each Corporation (each trade had its own Corporation with the right to representation in Parliament) there were representatives of capital and of labor with 'equal rights'. However, the Italian labor representatives were not selected by workers themselves, but were appointed by the PNF (National Fascist Party). And these representatives regularly kowtowed to the 'representatives of capital', who were the capitalists themselves, such as Giovanni Agnelli, Angelo Costa, Luigi Orlando, Guido Donegani, Achille Lauro and Antonio Pesenti. In Germany – as in Italy – in any labor dispute the employer was always right. This was not unlike Bolshevist Russia, where the company management appointed by the party was always in the right. In other words, Nazism, like Fascism and Communism, was a travesty that hurt the working class, despite the fact that Hitler continued to rail against "the bourgeoisie and the capitalists" in his speeches, Mussolini dedicated his mass meetings "to proletarian and Fascist Italy" and Stalin continuously spouted the myth of the working class.

Again copying the Italian model created by the Duce, who had invented the *Dopolavoro* (the leisure activities organization that provided inexpensive entertainment and vacations to workers and their families), Hitler came up with the motto – and the institution – *Kraft durch Freude* (Strength through Joy), offering trips, summer camps, theater performances, seaside and mountain vacations, and cruises, all at low cost. Strong in sports, particularly Alpine skiing, the organization eventually had seven million workers of both genders involved in sports and trained according to the myth of Aryan youth.

The decrees on labor policy culminated in the law of June 22, 1938, requiring each citizen to have a job and to accept the one assigned by the State through the Labor Offices. As a result the Third Reich completely eliminated unemployment. Another part of Hitler's labor policy was his promise that "each German worker will own an automobile," a pledge he made after commissioning the construction of a car he baptized the *Volkswagen*, the People's Car. At the time, in Germany there was 1 car for every 50 inhabitants (in the United States, the ratio was 1 to 5). Hitler pledged that "the Volkswagen will cost less than a thousand marks: 990," and he assigned engineer Ferdinand Porsche to oversee this project. As a result, in 1938 what the press and radio immediately defined as "the largest automobile factory in the world" was built in Fallersleben, near Braunschweig (later renamed Wolfsburg in honor of Hitler, who was nicknamed 'Wolf' by those closest to him). The factory's goal was to build 1.5 million Volkswagens a year, even more than Ford. The workers financed the undertaking by paying installments towards their Volkswagen. Unfortunately, the advent of the war doomed the project. To conclude this discussion of labor, from a historical standpoint it must be acknowledged that for many Germans it was worth relinquishing political freedom in exchange for the assurance of being employed indefinitely, and this is what the Labor Front managed to guarantee.

The Führer making a speech at the celebration of his 50th birthday at the Volkswagen ▶
factory in Fallersleben, near Wolfsburg. The car, designed and produced by Ferdinand Porsche, was commissioned by Hitler, who also gave it its name – People's Car.

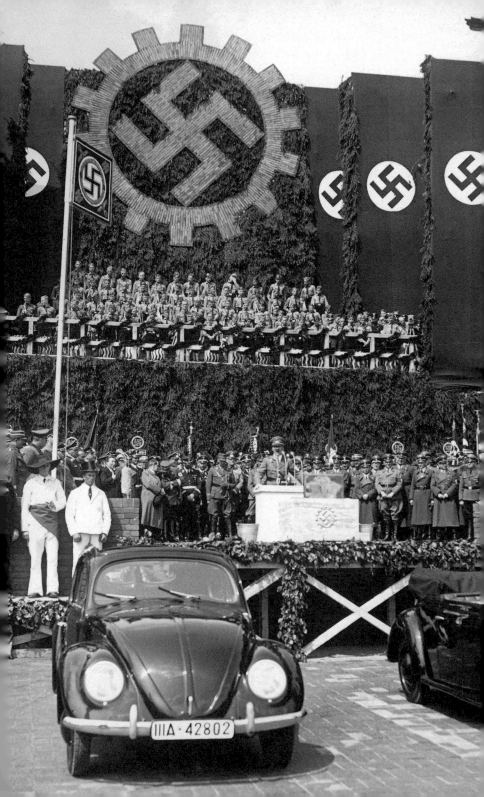

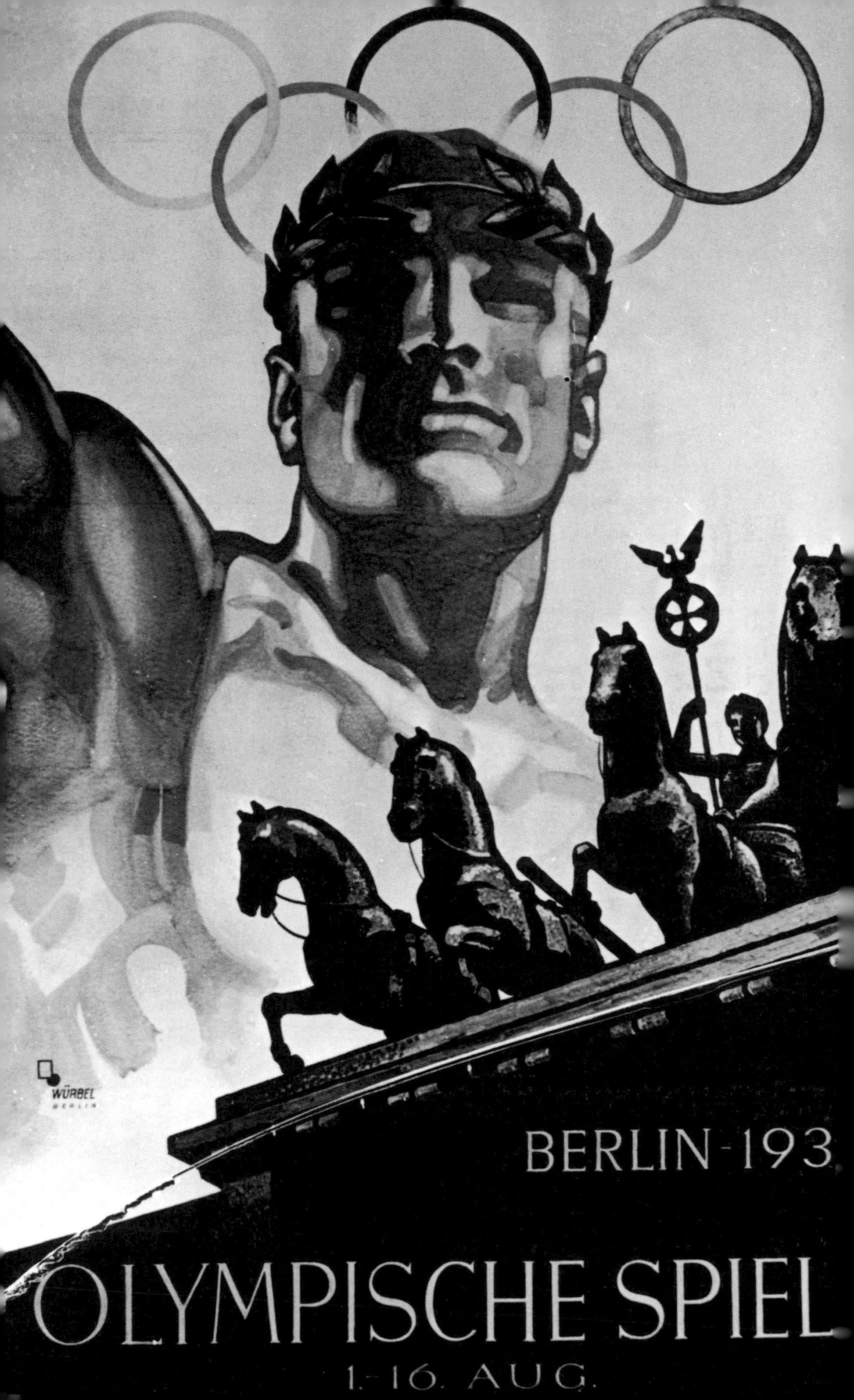
WÜRBEL
BERLIN
BERLIN-193
OLYMPISCHE SPIEL
1-16. AUG.

Since 1923, the Nazi Party conventions had always been held in Nuremberg, chosen because it had been an imperial city during the First Reich. With his rise to power, however, Hitler wanted to give these ceremonies a touch of grandeur that would dazzle the world. After the death of his personal architect, Munich native Ludwig Troost, Hitler called the young architect Albert Speer to his side. In Speer's book *Inside the Third Reich*, a fascinating work he wrote while serving his 20-year sentence at Spandau prison, he described Hitler's sway over him while he was studying in Heidelberg.

Hitler had admired monumental architecture ever since his early years in Vienna, and he gave Speer general instructions to transform Berlin, Munich and, above all, Nuremberg into imperial cities on a par with Vienna. In Nuremberg Speer mapped out an area of 183,000 square feet south of the city to be used for mass meetings, and he started planning impressive structures that would astonish the world. One of these projects involved a stadium with stone tiers that could seat 1 million people.

The renovated city of Nuremberg was unveiled for the 1934 *Parteitag*, shortly after the Night of the Long Knives, as a way of helping people forget the horrors of that night and stir the masses. Albert Speer had Zeppelin Field (which could hold 250,000 people) surrounded by 130 giant searchlights to create a "cathedral of light" visible as far as Frankfurt, 125 miles away. It was here that Leni Riefenstahl made her famous documentary *Triumph des Willens* (Triumph of the Will). Hitler himself had suggested the title to Riefenstahl, who was already a famous director. With 30 cameras, 120 assistants, the masterful use of light, spectacular frames and a rousing soundtrack, Leni created an audiovisual monument to the Third Reich, one that conveys powerful emo-

◀ *The poster of the 1936 Olympic Games, held in Berlin on August 1-16, with the participation of 52 nations. The Games, during which the black American Jesse Owens won four gold medals, were immortalized in Leni Riefenstahl's famous documentary* Olympia.

tions even today. Two years later, she would transcend her art with *Olympia*, a documentary on the Olympic Games.

Excluded from the 1920 and 1924 Olympics as a result of WWI, Germany was readmitted to the Games following the 1931 decision of the International Olympic Committee (IOC). The date was also set – the summer of 1936 – when Germany would have the honor of hosting the Games. The 1931 decision was a demonstration of trust towards a country that was once again democratic and responsible. Things had changed in the meantime, but despite enormous pressure the IOC was not willing to revoke the decision it had made. In March 1936, just months before the Olympic Games were scheduled to begin, the remilitarization of Rhineland, together with the ongoing persecution of Jews, led many countries to boycott the Olympics. Hitler remedied this at the last minute by including several Jewish athletes in the organizing committee. As a result, 52 countries participated in the event, including the United States, France and Great Britain.

On July 20, 1936 the first relay left Greek soil – from Olympia – to head to Berlin. Three thousand runners took turns in the torch relay, which was covered by journalists around the world. There was enormous enthusiasm when the relay passed through Vienna, as hundreds of thousands of voices cried "Heil Hitler!" and this feverish crescendo was captured on film by Leni Riefenstahl and her expert team of movie operators. On August 1, when the torch was carried into the Olympic sports complex in Berlin, 100,000 arms were outstretched in the Nazi salute, as the *Hindenburg*, the 804-foot-long dirigible, hovered in the air.

Hitler obviously could not prevent Jewish fencing champion Helene Mayer nor black track champion Jesse Owens from winning, but the German athletes took plenty of gold medals, winning 33. The United States took second place with 24 gold medals, four of which were won by Owens alone.

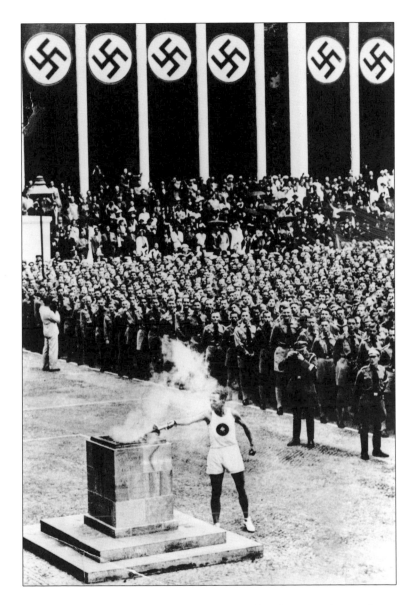

The inauguration of the 1936 Olympic Games. The Olympic torch was taken to the Lustgarten of Berlin from Mt. Olympus in Greece by a relay of more than 3000 runners.

THE THIRD REICH
CHALLENGES
THE WORLD

«My intention," stated Adolf Hitler in his speech in Berlin on January 30, 1941, "was to abrogate the Treaty of Versailles: I said and wrote this thousands of times." Breaching the Treaty of Versailles meant rearmament, first of all, and then regaining the lands that had been lost: the Saar, Alsace-Lorraine, the colonies, Danzig and the other eastern regions ceded to Poland. But the plans that Hitler outlined in *Mein Kampf*, in dozens of interviews and in hundreds of speeches went beyond that. They envisaged the annexation of "lands where German is spoken" (thus Austria and Sudetenland, but not South Tyrol, because it was more important keep Fascist Italy as a friend and ally) and the conquest of *Lebensraum*, or 'living space', which could not be achieved except at the expense of the territories to the east. To deal with population growth at the end of the 19th century, other countries such as Italy and Poland had relied on massive emigration to the United States. Not Germany. "We demand land," announced Hitler, "to support our people and make room for our excessive population." Someone had proposed limiting births, but this idea was rejected imme-

◄ *Benito Mussolini and Adolf Hitler during their first official meeting in Venice on June 14, 1934. On October 23, 1936, after the tension with Great Britain due to Italy's war against Ethiopia, Italy and Germany signed the Rome-Berlin Axis, which on May 22, 1939 became the Pact of Steel.*

diately and decisively. It was a 'defeatist' idea. Besides, everyone knew that, according to Nazi dogma, the perfect couple had to have at least four children.

The move to rearm began with the *Friedensrede*, the 'peace speech' that Hitler gave at the Reichstag on May 17, 1933, during which he addressed the participants of the World Disarmament Conference that was about to convene in Geneva. He said, "War is unbounded madness. We have long been disarmed. Now it is up to you. We are not asking to rearm, but for others to disarm." Unfortunately, his proposal was rejected outright, particularly by France. Following the declarations and stances taken by the victors of the Great War, on October 14, 1933 Hitler thus announced that Germany was withdrawing from the Conference and from the League of Nations. "It is with pain, not rage, that national dignity forces me to take this step. I have already said that war is a monster to be avoided, but peace cannot be the perpetuation of war. For 15 years, the German people have hoped that the end of the war would mean the end of hatred and enmity. They have unfortunately waited in vain." He expressed the same concepts in an interview he granted to Ward Price of the *Daily Mail*, which was discussed around the world. At this point, he wanted the consent of the people and he called on the Germans to express this in a plebiscite held on November 12, 1933, at the same time as the Reichstag elections. Ninety-six percent of those with the right to vote went to the polls, and 95% of them agreed with Germany's withdrawal from the League of Nations. At the same time, the sole list of deputies to be elected was approved by 92% of those voting. In reality, the entire country backed its Führer.

At this point, rearmament could be implemented in broad daylight, though mitigated by an appeasement policy that culminated in a ten-year nonaggression pact that was signed with Poland, governed by Marshal Pilsudski, on January 26, 1934 – despite the fact that Poland was hated by all German Nationalists for having incorporated Danzig, the province of Posen and part of Silesia, thereby detaching Eastern Prussia from the Reich.

The second stage of this plan – the union of all German lands under a single flag – proved far more difficult for Hitler to carry out. In Vienna, the Austrian National Socialist Party founded by thirty-year-old Alfred Eduard Frauenfeld was flourishing. By the beginning of 1934, it already had 40,000 members in the capital alone and it openly demanded *Anschluss*, Germany's annexation of Austria. However, Czechoslovakia, backed by its alliance with France, and Italy, the power that had declared itself the protector of Austria and Hungary, opposed the plan. Austrian Prime Minister Engelbert Dollfuss and Benito Mussolini were personal friends, and Dollfuss and his family even spent their vacation at Mussolini's seaside house in Riccione. Through Mussolini's initiative, on February 17, 1934 Great Britain, France and Italy issued a joint declaration proclaiming "Austria's right to independence and territorial integrity." One month later to the day, Mussolini and the representatives of Austria and Hungary signed the Rome Protocols, which reconfirmed the political dependency of the two Danube states on Italy. Not by chance, the Venice meeting of June 14, 1934 between Mussolini and Hitler served to underscore the German leader's evident sense of inferiority and near embarrassment in the company of his Italian counterpart.

Given this background, one can easily imagine Mussolini's astonishment and rage when, on the evening of July 15, 1934, he heard that Vienna had fallen into the hands of Nazi insurrectionists who had burst into the government building, shot Dollfuss and announced over the radio that General Anton von Rintelen (who was wholly unaware of this) had been appointed Chancellor. At the time Dollfuss' wife and children were the Duce's guests for the summer holidays, and they had the traumatic experience of learning that the Austrian leader had died in the hospital a few hours after being shot by the Nazis.

While this was happening, Hitler was at the theater in Bayreuth, attending a performance of *Das Rheingold* seated next to Winifred Wagner. Hitler's adjutants Schaub and Brückner kept coming into their box to update him minute by minute. When the opera was over, Hitler pretended that nothing had happened and went to a restaurant, feigning total disinterest in the dramatic events underway in Vienna.

The putsch was squelched after three days of armed conflict in Vienna, Styria and Carinthia. The rebel leaders and supporters fled to Germany, while Mussolini sent two divisions to the Brenner Pass and guaranteed the Austrian government his complete support against any German military aggression. In the face of Italy's reaction, Hitler backed down. He delivered Dollfuss' killers to Vienna, removed Theo Habicht, the NSDAP inspector for Austria, and replaced the German ambassador in Vienna with Franz von Papen, who was more agreeable to the Austrians because he was Catholic, conservative and 'anti-Nazi'.

On March 4, 1935, Great Britain launched an alert through a declaration of the Foreign Ministry: "Germany is rearming on a large scale, in full violation of the terms of the Versailles Treaty." At this point, Hitler decided to admit this openly, going so far as to accentuate rearmament in order to sound out international reactions. With a flurry of diplomatic notes, Berlin informed foreign powers that it had reestablished its Air Force and, with the note of March 16, 1935, it added that Germany was about to reintroduce the draft in order to create an army of 36 divisions: 550,000 men.

This was blatant provocation, but the only reactions were a string of verbal protests and a conference convened in Stresa on April 11, 1935 by the League of Nations (Mussolini arrived there piloting a seaplane that 'landed' on the waters of the lake). The conference closed with the usual condemnation of this action and with renewed assurance of Austria's independence. Only France took concrete steps, signing a pact of mutual military assistance with the USSR. Hitler gave a crafty speech at the Reichstag on May 21, reassuring everyone of the Germans' desire for peace. His were lofty words that repeatedly alluded to reason and justice ("Whoever lights the torch of war in Europe can wish for nothing but chaos.") but also specifically referred to the principle of the "self-determination of nations" contained in U.S. President Woodrow Wilson's Fourteen Points.

However, the unanimity achieved – at least on paper – among the major powers (Great Britain, France, the United States and Italy) at the Stresa Conference soon crumbled, when Joachim von Ribbentrop, Hitler's special envoy to London, signed a naval agreement with the English government whereby Germany pledged that it would not exceed 35% of Britain's naval forces. Ribbentrop, a former wine merchant who had married the daughter of the champagne king Henkel, enjoyed the Führer's complete trust. Hitler had granted him special powers that allowed him to circumvent the ambassador and even the German Foreign Minister, Konstantin von Neurath, whom he had set out to replace and actually did so soon afterwards. England, in turn, had acted without consulting her allies, offending France and, above all, Italy – the quintessential naval power – and these two countries considered the agreement an affront and an act of disloyalty.

Heedless and self-confident, Hitler marched on. His successful exploits, particularly in foreign policy, climaxed with the party convention held in Nuremberg on September 15 and 16, 1935. For the occasion, the Führer convened a special session of the Reichstag, to be held in what was considered the 'moral capital' of Nazism, where he submitted the anti-Jewish legislation (which was unanimously approved) that became known as the "Nuremberg Laws" and "laws of racial purity". The former stripped German Jews of their citizenship, banned marriages between Jews and non-Jewish Germans and, among other things – in a crescendo of 'prudishness' – prohibited Jews from hiring German women under the age of 34 as house servants. For all intents and purposes, the laws to safeguard the race also authorized the use of euthanasia for mental patients, who had already been subject to sterilization following the law passed on July 14, 1933.

In the meantime, independently of Hitler's own intentions, a move on the international chessboard was about to pave the way for his plans. The chilly relations between Italy and Great Britain, which began with the Ribbentrop Agreement, turned into open hostility following London's request to the League of Nations to apply economic sanctions against Rome for having invaded Ethiopia with the aim of creating a new colony in East Africa. With his initiative, which was accepted in Geneva, British Prime Minister Stanley Baldwin turned Mussolini into an enemy, pushing him straight into Hitler's arms. And Hitler, in turn, did not hesitate to manifest Germany's full solidarity with the Duce. In the fall of 1935, the possibility of a Rome-Berlin Axis was discussed for the first time.

Hitler did not hesitate to make the most of his new and important diplomatic success. The opportunity arrived when, on February 27, 1936, the Lower House of the French Parliament ratified the Franco-Soviet treaty of mutual aid. Hitler's response was to remilitarize the Rhineland, that is, the German territories west of the Rhine that, based on the Versailles Treaty, were to remain permanently demilitarized (and that also left the French borders defenseless). On the morning of March 7, 1936, a force of 35,000 German soldiers headed to Aachen, Trier and Saarbrücken, welcomed by a delirious crowd. At that time, Hitler completely ignored the recommendations of his Army Chief of Staff, General Ludwig Beck, to move cautiously and, despite Beck's opinion to the contrary, he ordered the soldiers to erect a chain of permanent fortifications immediately. He had taken a gamble. Years later, he would admit, "The two days that followed our march into the Rhineland were the most nerve-wracking of my life."

As was his habit following a major decision, Hitler called upon the people to express their opinion with a plebiscite. He dissolved the Reichstag and called for new elections, which were held on March 29, 1936. Ninety-nine percent of eligible voters went to the polls, and 98.8% of these voters approved the sole list of deputies, with 540,000 'nays' versus 45 million 'yeas'.

A short time later, a dramatic international event occurred that helped strengthen the bond that was being forged between Germany and Italy. Civil war broke out in Spain on July 17 and General Francisco Franco, who led the uprising against the republican government in Madrid, asked Italy and Germany for military aid. Hitler complied, sending materiel, instructors and the Condor Legion, which specialized in air strikes of the government's positions. Italy sent combat divisions that, in March 1937, numbered 70,000 regulars. Italians and Germans thus found themselves on the same side of the fence in an ideological conflict between Fascism and anti-Fascist forces – a brutal war that would ultimately claim 1 million lives.

In August 1936, Ribbentrop was named ambassador to London and was assigned to forge stronger ties not only with Great Britain but also with Japan, with an eye to isolating Germany's two historic enemies, France and Russia. Hitler's plan was to create a front against international Communism, hopefully with the support of both these powers. However, he would succeed only with Japan, with which Germany signed the Anti-Comintern Pact in Berlin that November.

During the September 1936 Nuremberg Rally Hitler announced his "four-year plan" that, spearheaded by Goering, focused the sights of the German economy on a single objective: preparing for war. The elimination of unemployment, a doubled gross domestic product and the revaluation of the mark could have ensured a high standard of living for everyone. But war expenditures had top priority. In his speech of January 30, 1937 Hitler demanded that the colonies be returned to Germany. In the meantime, he continued to woo Mussolini more and more insistently, inviting him to a triumphal trip to Germany that began on September 23, 1937 and ended with a speech that Mussolini gave in German before a crowd of 1 million in Berlin. This was a gigantic display of power, the apotheosis of which was the Führer's speech: "The Duce is one of those men, unique through the ages, who do not succumb to history but are the makers of history." The upshot came on November 6, 1937, when Italy joined the Anti-Comintern Pact and – simultaneously and inevitably – yielded on the Austrian question. In short, for Hitler the coast to Vienna was clear. At the September 1937 Rally, he gave a very harsh speech that was a full-fledged prologue to war. He compared the clash between National Socialism and Bolshevism to the historic one between Christianity and Islam. "Communism," he cried, "is none other than the world plot of the Jews orchestrated by Moscow. The blind statesmen of London and Paris do not understand that the Jewish gang in Moscow wants to extend its brutal dictatorship across Western Europe and around the world." It was the prelude to action.

The principle of *Lebensraum*, the 'living space' that had long been paraded about and demanded, was put into practice on November 5, 1937, when the Führer convened a meeting at the Chancellor's Office with War Minister Blomberg, General von Fritsch, Commander in Chief of the Army, Admiral Raeder, Commander in Chief of the Navy, Reichsmarschall Goering,

Commander in Chief of the Air Force, and Foreign Minister Neurath. Colonel Friedrich Hossbach, Hitler's military adjutant, sat in a corner of the room, quietly and discreetly jotting down what was being said. His annotations would prove to be a valuable historical account. Hitler announced that the time had come to augment the living space of the German people, to the detriment of the lands to the east. He added that this indubitably entailed the risk of war, observing that the danger did not come from the USSR, but rather "from our traditional enemies steeped in hatred: France and Great Britain." It was essential to be prepared to face their reaction. How? The most practical hypothesis was sudden action against Austria and Czechoslovakia, once the defenses to the west had been reinforced. Italy, Poland and Russia would certainly not lift a finger. "The Wehrmacht," he bantered, thinking of the new Austrian recruits, "will have twelve more divisions. As to Czechoslovakia," he concluded, "Great Britain and France are unlikely to risk a war in her defense." Once again, he was right on target.

CHAPTER 8

1938-39:
THE FATAL YEARS

At the end of the summit meeting of November 5, 1937, when Hitler announced his decision to use armed forces to annex Austria and Sudetenland, War Minister Blomberg and Werner von Fritsch, Commander in Chief of the Army, manifested their reservations and fears, declaring that they were totally against risking a war with Great Britain and France. In turn, Foreign Minister Neurath avowed that the Führer's forecast of a conflict between France and Italy, which would give Germany greater freedom of action, was completely wrong. Hitler did not take this well. According to Alan Bullock, those who were not willing to follow him blindly had to leave their posts. Less than three months later, the three "internal opponents" were forced out, just as – on September 5 – the powerful and influential banker Hjalmar Schacht had been forced to resign as Minister of Economics, despite the fact that he had enabled Germany to rearm without triggering inflation. Now, however, Schacht feared that Germany's foreign trade would be boycotted by the other European countries.

Moreover, the unacknowledgeable pact that was established between the Generalität and Nazism on the eve of the Night of

◄ *After the Munich Conference held on September 30, 1938 the Sudetenland was ceded to Germany. Here Hitler is seen crossing the old frontier on October 4, 1938, welcomed by the leaders of the Sudeten National Socialist Party.*

the Long Knives in 1934 was beginning to reveal its limitations. The generals were not prepared for the hellish pace of Hitler's rearmament policy: 4000 officers were not nearly enough to instruct millions of recruits. And then there was the fact that the Führer had created 36 divisions without even discussing this with the Joint Chiefs of Staff. Likewise, the remilitarization of the Rhineland was decided overnight and General Erich von Manstein was forced to draw up the occupation plan in the space of an afternoon. The upper ranks did not share the Führer's strategic moves, such as the mutual aid pacts with Poland and Japan, and the friendship with Italy. They looked down on the Poles and the Italians, and instead of Japan they would have preferred the USSR, whose creation had been made possible partly thanks to the funds the Kaiser's General Staff had channeled to facilitate Lenin's revolt in 1917. Lastly, they feared the bugbear of a war on two fronts (French and Russian) and, above all, they were coldly contemptuous of the SS troops led by Himmler and his chief lieutenant Reinhard Heydrich, who had been expelled from the Navy officer corps in 1920 for conduct unbecoming an officer.

'Settling accounts' with Blomberg was effected in a base and treacherous manner, much like a police operation. The sixty-year-old field marshal, widowed since 1932, had fallen in love with one of his secretaries, the pretty young Erna Gruhn. Through Goering he had requested Hitler's approval to marry the girl. It did not take the Nazi leaders long to discover that the Berlin police had a dossier on the girl, who had a record as a prostitute. Instead of informing their government colleague, Goering and Hitler kept the embarrassing document under wraps and even attended the wedding as Blomberg's witnesses. They waited for the couple to leave on January 13, 1938 for their honeymoon in Capri and then they launched a vile campaign, spreading rumors through anonymous phone calls to high-ranking Wehrmacht officers and pretending to have unexpectedly discovered Erna Gruhn's dossier. During the honeymoon, Blomberg was notified that his elderly mother had passed away. When he returned to Berlin for the funeral, Goering went to Blomberg's office and showed him the file on Erna's past, informing him that he – and, above all, the Führer – were convinced they had been tricked into agreeing to stand in at the wedding as Blomberg's witnesses. Desperate, Blomberg swore that he knew nothing of his wife's past and said he was willing to divorce her immediately. But Goering replied, "At this point, that is no longer enough. The entire officer corps has heard about this and demands your resignation as minister." Blomberg had no choice. Nevertheless, he refused to commit suicide, as was suggested to him by zealous officers close to the regime. He died on March 13, 1946 in Nuremberg, where the victors had locked him in a prison cell – arbitrarily, as it turned out, because he had been called there not as a defendant, but as a witness.

Now that Blomberg, the most important protector of the Commander in Chief of the Army, Colonel General Werner von Fritsch, had been eliminated, it was time to get rid of the latter. A baron, Fritsch was detested because of his hostility towards the Nazis, particularly Himmler and his SS, and he was even haughty with the Führer himself. William Shirer provides an eloquent description of Fritsch: "On March 1, 1935, the day Germany took over the Saar, I stood in the stand next to Fritsch.... in the reviewing stand at Saarbruecken for some time before the parade started. Although he scarcely knew me, except as one of the many American correspondents in Berlin, he poured out a running fire of sarcastic remarks about the SS, the party and the various Nazi leaders from Hitler on down. He did not disguise his contempt for them all."

Fritsch was accused of homosexuality, a crime punishable pursuant to Article 175 of the penal code. The SS created a dossier with the testimony of a police informer who declared that, on a street in Berlin, he had personally witnessed sexual relations between the general and a homosexual named Bavarian Joe. The dossier was delivered to Goering, who handed it over to Hitler. There was even a secret confrontation between Fritsch and his accuser in Hitler's presence. Indignant, the general never opened his mouth. When Hitler asked him to resign, Fritsch responded, "Never! I demand a trial by a military court of honor."

When he returned to Bendlerstrasse, he spoke to the Chief of the Army General Staff Ludwig Beck. Equally incensed, Beck urged him to carry out an immediate coup d'état, but there was no way to guarantee its outcome. Hours of terrible tension followed. Everyone among the highest ranks of the Army heard how Fritsch had been set up, and many hoped for a repeat of the Night of the Long Knives, this time against Himmler and the SS. But Hitler forestalled everyone. On February 4, 1938 he called a Cabinet meeting to approve a decree that began with the words, "Henceforth, the Führer shall personally command all the armed forces." As a result, the rank of *Höchstkriegsherr* or Supreme Commander was created. The sixteen highest-ranking generals, included Erwin von Witzleben and Beck, were immediately sidelined and 44 other generals were transferred to lesser posts. The War Ministry was abolished and in its place Hitler created the OKW (*Oberkommando der Wehrmacht* or Supreme Armed Forces Command), which was to be led by one of his closest collaborators, General Wilhelm Keitel. To placate Goering's unvoiced but evident resentment, the high-sounding title of *Reichsmarschall* was invented for him, and the press was informed that Blomberg and Fritsch had resigned for health reasons. General Walther von Brauchitsch succeeded Fritsch as head of the Army, whereas the Navy (Admiral Raeder) and the Air Force (Goering) had long been in the grips of Nazi ideology by this time. During that same fateful Cabinet meeting of February 4,

Foreign Minister Neurath was replaced by Ribbentrop, order executor Walther Funk was appointed Minister of Economics, and the three most important German ambassadors – none of whom were Nazis, namely Ulrich von Hassell (Rome), Herbert von Dirksen (Tokyo) and Franz von Papen (Vienna) – were replaced with yesmen. Thus, all the persons Hindenburg had put in key positions to curb Nazi excesses had been eliminated in a single stroke.

The moment for Vienna and the *Anschluss* had arrived. Throughout 1937, the Austrian Nazis had organized violent actions in order to force the police to carry out harsh repression that would justify German intervention to protect its Nazi comrades. In the early months of 1938, the maneuver had led to a series of sensational arrests of Nazis accused of attempting to overthrow the government. At this point, Hitler asked Chancellor Schuschnigg to meet him at the Berghof for a summit. Born in the Italian town of Riva del Garda to a family of officers from the Tyrol area, Kurt von Schuschnigg had become involved in politics by chance. When he returned to civilian life following WWI, he went to work as an attorney, but Dollfuss needed a dynamic War Minister. The former Alpenjäger officer, who was a member of Dollfuss' party, the *Heimatsfront*, was just the man. When Dollfuss was assassinated, the office of Chancellor fell to Schuschnigg. The former attorney, who was just 37 years old in 1934, had come to enjoy politics and was a brilliant speaker. The Patriotic Front, the only party allowed in Austria, followed him en masse. Everyone was convinced that he was the best man to counter Hitler's expansionist ambitions.

Schuschnigg arrived at the Berghof on the afternoon of February 13, 1938, but the welcome he received was far different from what he may have imagined. Hitler was surrounded by his generals and had meticulously studied a diabolical plan to weaken his young adversary's resolve. Schuschnigg, a sophisticated and highly educated man, suddenly found himself treated like a beggar. To break the ice, upon his arrival the Austrian Chancellor commented on the marvelous view from the windows of the Berghof, to which Hitler replied, "I did not call you here to discuss the weather." A few minutes later, with an angry wave of his hand he ordered Schuschnigg to put out the cigarette he had just lit. For over three hours, the Austrian had to submit to the harsh verbal onslaught of the German dictator, who accused him and his country of high treason. At the end of this philippic, the Führer listed the terms of his ultimatum (appointment of Nazi leader Seyss-Inquart as Minister of the Interior, amnesty for all the Nazis who had been sentenced, the immediate release of those arrested, German officers at the head of the Austrian army), but Schuschnigg played for time. First he had to inform the President of the Austrian Republic, Wilhelm Miklas. And at this point, Hitler sprung his trap. Beside himself with rage, he shouted, "Keitel, come here at once!" Schuschnigg, convinced that Hitler was about to order the invasion of Austria, signed the document accepting Germany's demands. Upon his return to Vienna, however, he announced that popular approval was required and called for a plebiscite on March 13. Hitler's reaction was swift. After obtaining the 'understanding' of Mussolini (the only person Hitler feared would react strongly), he ordered Schuschnigg to resign. To avoid a bloodbath at the Bavarian border, the Chancellor agreed and President Miklas placed Seyss-Inquart in charge of the government. It was all in vain. At dawn on Saturday, March 12, the Wehrmacht crossed the Austrian border. That afternoon, Hitler spoke to the cheering crowd in Linz, the city where he had grown up. Then he headed to Vienna, where he was welcomed in triumph. Schuschnigg ended up in prison, where he was held until the end of the war.

March 13, 1938: a spectacular parade of German automobiles and military vehicles in ▶ front of the Vienna City Hall marks the realization of the Anschluss, *the annexation of Austria by the Third Reich.*

It was now the turn of the Sudetenland. On May 30, 1938 the Supreme Commander sent secret instructions to the OKW, which started with the words, "It is my intention to crush Czechoslovakia with military action by October 1 of this year." The facts would show that Hitler did not choose this date arbitrarily. Three million people of German language, culture and traditions lived in the Sudeten region of Czechoslovakia. United under the banner of the SDP (Sudeten German Party), led by Konrad Henlein, they represented a powerful minority group. Called to Berlin, Henlein received orders to make unacceptable demands to the government in Prague. The Czech president, Edvard Benes, held fast, hoping for the support of his two allies, France and Great Britain, but he was deceiving himself. Great Britain was the first to betray the alliance, sending Lord Runciman to 'investigate' the accusations of violence and abuse of power of which the Sudeten accused the Czech government. In the meantime, Berlin urged Poland and Hungary to demand the return of the Czech territories that were home to Polish and Hungarian minorities.

A violent speech by Hitler at the Nuremberg Rally on September 12, 1938 roused people's spirits and sparked a revolt in the Sudetenland. Prague proclaimed martial law. Henlein and the heads of the SDP fled to Germany. At this point, invasion seemed to be around the corner, but both France and Great Britain were unwilling to get involved in the war that would inevitably follow. British Prime Minister Neville Chamberlain thus decided to step in, convincing Benes to cede the Sudetenland to Germany without a struggle. The news, delivered personally to the Führer by Chamberlain, who went to the Berghof on September 22, outraged Hitler. He could see his whole plan going up in smoke, for he wanted to take over all of Czechoslovakia and not just the Sudetenland. In his speech of September 26 at the Sportpalast in Berlin, he raged against Benes: "There is no Czech nation! It is a falsehood of history!" This was an enormous slap in the face for Great Britain. The world waited with bated breath and the press heralded another world war.

It was at this point that Mussolini stepped in, promoting a summit meeting of the major powers. Held in Munich, the conference began at half past noon on September 29, 1938, with Hitler, Mussolini, Chamberlain and French Prime Minister Daladier in attendance. At dawn on September 30, an agreement was reached: the following day, October 1, the German army would enter Czech territory, solely to take possession of the Sudetenland. Once again, the date planned by the Führer was being respected.

Mussolini was praised by the world press as "the savior of peace." As his train left for Rome, hailed by jubilant crowds as it passed, the Czech Prime Minister, General Jan Sirovy, went on the radio to broadcast to the people that the government had accepted Munich's terms. In his announcement, he noted, "It would be easier for me to die than to have to speak to you. But we were abandoned. We stand alone." In London, Churchill took the floor at the House of Commons to rail that Hitler had not merely stolen his food, he had managed to have it served to him on a platter. "Shame on you!" cried Churchill. Just a few days later, Hungary and Poland also obtained permission to annex the Czech territories they wanted. Benes resigned and requested political asylum in the United States. He was succeeded by General Sirovy, but he too resigned on November 30, 1938, leaving the government in the hands of Emil Hácha.

The respite enjoyed by Hácha and his collaborators was very brief. On March 12, 1939, bloody disorders broke out simultaneously in Prague and Bratislava, ably fomented by agents from Berlin and leaving many dead. Hácha proclaimed martial law and ordered the arrest of Nazi sympathizers in Prague and of the entire regional government of Slovakia, led by Monsignor Tiso. Only the priest managed to escape and a German plane took him to Berlin. Hitler received him at the Reich Chancellery and announced,

"I've decided to be done with Czechoslovakia. Tomorrow you will return to Bratislava and proclaim Slovakia as an independent and sovereign state. Germany will immediately give its official recognition." As soon as the astonished monsignor had been sent on his way, the Führer phoned the Czech ambassador and shouted, "I want the President of the Republic and the head of the Czech government here at once! This is an ultimatum. If they do not arrive by tomorrow afternoon, I will order the Luftwaffe to raze Prague to the ground!" It was the evening of March 14. Within a few hours, Hácha and his prime minister were before Hitler and a wretched nighttime discussion began. Hácha fainted and was revived by Hitler's physician, Dr. Theodor Morell. At 4 a.m. on March 15, Hácha signed Czechoslovakia's capitulation ("I place the destiny of my people in the Führer's hands.") and then promptly fainted again. When he came to, he phoned the commander of the army in Prague and ordered him not to oppose the entry of the German troops in Czech territory. A few minutes later (this detail is reported in David Irving's book *Hitler's War*), the Führer entered the office where his two secretaries, Christa Schröder and Gerda Daranowsky, had been up all night. Patting his cheeks, he exclaimed, "Girls, come here. One on this side and one on the other: a kiss for each of you. This is the greatest day of my life!"

At 6 a.m., the Wehrmacht invaded Czechoslovakia. Four hours later, the German fanfares resounded in Venceslao Square, in the heart of Prague. The following morning, Hitler sat in a Mercedes and rode through the streets of the loveliest city in Europe, looking out in mockery over the silent crowd that, glaring in powerless hatred, was crushed between the streets and houses by a double cordon of storm troopers. Hitler entered the castle of Hradcany, the ancient seat of the Bohemian kings, which had flags with swastikas fluttering from its windows. Here he proclaimed the annexation of Bohemia and Moravia to the Reich. That same morning, with the munificent gesture of the satisfied conqueror, he allowed Polish troops to occupy and annex Silesia, and permitted the Hungarians to do the same with Ruthenia.

And now it was Poland's turn, but first Hitler had to finalize two masterly strokes of foreign and military policy: an ironclad alliance with Fascist Italy and a nonaggression pact with Communist Russia, to avoid risking war on two fronts. This was particularly important since Chamberlain, evidently ruing the fact that he had acquiesced in Munich, announced to the House of Commons on March 31 that Great Britain was "ready to guarantee the independence of Poland." And France readily backed England, marking the end of the policy of appeasement and deciding, finally, that one could also "die for Danzig."

The first move was a success, partly thanks to an article – as providential as it was vituperative – by an American journalist. The article managed to irritate Mussolini and push him to adhere to Hitler's pressing requests. The Pact of Steel was officially signed in Berlin on May 22, 1939. Article III of the pact provided that each of the two parties would go to war to aid its ally if it became involved in a situation of belligerence with another power.

The following day, Hitler called his military leaders to the Chancellery and announced that war had become inevitable (a statement in the notes taken by Colonel Rudolf Schmundt, the Führer's adjutant). Hitler specified that the pretext would be provided by the claim for Danzig and its free territory, but that the true purpose would be the conquest of the Baltic states and of Poland itself, not only to take over its abundant harvests "indispensable for the survival and progress of the German people," but also to exploit local manpower at low cost. "We cannot expect a repetition of the Czech operation," continued Hitler. "This time there will be war." He then proceeded with a lucid announcement of his grand strategic operations, all of which then came to pass: occupation of the Netherlands and Belgium, victory over France, and the isolation and subsequent air attack on England. Lastly, there was a peremptory order that everything was to be kept top secret, even from Italy and Japan. The time had come to draw Stalin and Russia on his side. This operation was conducted in two phases. First of all, Ribbentrop obtained Lithuania's peaceful return of Memelland (taken from East Prussia by the Versailles Treaty) and three nonaggression agreements were signed with Lithuania, Latvia and Estonia. Then he embarked on a series of commercial agreements with the USSR, which kept the two diplomatic corps engaged for the months of June and July 1939.

On August 20, through a personal message to Stalin, Hitler requested a meeting between Ribbentrop and the new Soviet Foreign Minister Vjaceslav Molotov. Stalin agreed and the two met in Moscow on August 23. That evening, Stalin drank repeated toasts "to the Führer's health," pouring himself drinks from a bottle of vodka that a German officer in the retinue furtively discovered contained only water. In turn, Ribbentrop reported that he felt as if he were "among comrades."

The following morning, the two ministers signed the Nazi-Soviet Pact, which was divided into two parts. One (which was announced to the international press) involved the nonaggression agreement. The other (which was kept secret) called for the partition of Poland, the assignment of Lithuania to the German sphere of influence and the assignment of Latvia, Estonia and Finland to the Russian one.

In Rome, Mussolini immediately understood that war was at hand and, recalling Article III of the Pact of Steel, hastily informed the Führer that Italy would be unable to provide Germany with any military aid in the event of an attack by France and Great Britain. As an alternative, the Duce offered to act as a mediator between Germany and Poland. Hitler, who had no use for Italy's military support, politely declined the offer.

Time was running short: Hitler needed a pretext to invade Poland. And this was meticulously organized by Himmler's right-hand man, Reinhard Heydrich. To stage the operation, he chose the German radio station of Gleiwitz, along the Polish border. On the night of August 30, seven men – common criminals who had been sentenced to death by German courts – were led into the building, which had been cleared of employees and technicians. Two of them were forced to wear Polish army uniforms. A few minutes later, an SS platoon, also dressed in Polish uniforms, burst into the rooms and, with a burst of machine-gun fire, killed the unfortunate pair. An accomplice, whose mother tongue was Polish, then read an appeal over the radio, urging the Polish people to rise up and fight against Germany.

A few hours later, as the foreign reporters were taken to the radio station to see the massacre with their own eyes, Hitler boomed over the radio, "Poland will pay dearly for this crime!" At 6 o'clock on the morning of Friday, September 1, 1939 the armored divisions of the Wehrmacht broke through the blockades along the entire border with Poland.

England gave Germany two ultimatums, one on the evening of September 1 and the other at 9 a.m. on September 3. The latter warned that if the German troops were not ordered to withdraw from Polish territory immediately, Great Britain would consider itself "at war with Germany as of 11 o'clock." Hitler and his closest collaborators listened to the note, read by the interpreter Dr. Paul Schmidt, in stony silence. Only Goering interrupted to exclaim, "If we lose this war, may God have mercy on us."

At 11:15 a.m. that Sunday, September 3, 1939 His Majesty's Foreign Minister, Lord Halifax, delivered the declaration of war to the German chargé d'affaires in London. A few minutes later, the same thing occurred in Paris. The most terrible war in the history of humanity had begun.

CHAPTER 9

HITLER'S WAR

I n accordance with the secret clauses of the iniquitous
Ribbentrop-Molotov pact, on September 17, 1939 the
Soviet Union invaded eastern Poland, which was already
desperately trying to resist the German advance. In only a few
days the Red Army captured 200,000 soldiers and 10,000 officers,
massacring the latter soon afterwards at Katyn. The Polish army
resisted frantically until September 27, when the Wehrmacht
took Warsaw. The army under General Sikorski was annihilated,
suffering 70,000 deaths, 133,000 wounded and 700,000 prisoners of war in a matter of days. Germany showed the world that
it had become a lethal war machine. The triumphant Führer was
cheered when, on the evening of November 8, 1939, he appeared
at the Bürgerbräukeller in Munich to celebrate the anniversary
of the abortive 1923 Putsch. No one could have imagined that a
bomb was waiting for him – but the defeated Poles had nothing
to do with it.

The instigator of the assassination attempt, the recluse Johann
Elser, was a former member of Communist action teams and a
worker at the Dornier airplane factory in Wilhelmshaven. He

◄ *Hitler with the Eiffel Tower, the symbol of Paris, in the background after the Wehrmacht
entered the French capital on June 14, 1940. France officially surrendered at Compiègne
on June 22.*

was captured a few days later and sent to the concentration camp at Sachsenhausen, where he was assassinated in 1945 by the SS shortly before the arrival of the Americans. The bomb exploded at 9:20 p.m., killing 7 and wounding 63, but Hitler escaped the blast because he had left the hall soon after finishing his speech. He was expected in Berlin the next day for an appointment with Charles Bedaux, a trusted colleague of Edward, Duke of Windsor (the former Edward VIII of England, known for his Nazi sympathies). Bedaux was to furnish the Führer with documentation on the French defenses from Calais to the Maginot Line. This information had been collected by the duke during inspections made as a general in the British Expeditionary Force in France. Furthermore, Hitler supposedly asked Bedaux to install his commander during World War I, Lieutenant Rosenbusch (a Jew), in one of Bedaux's companies, Bedaux Associates, in Istanbul.

Indeed, those months of stasis on the Western Front – the international press referred it as the *drôle de guerre* (strange war) phony war and *Sitzkrieg* (sitting war) – were used by both sides to collect as much information as possible on the potential and deployment of the enemy. However, a real war was fought off the Scottish coast and in the waters of South America, where German submarines and 'pocket battleships' attacked British warships and passenger ships flying the British flag.

The illusion lasted seven months. At the beginning of April 1940, Hitler took the initiative and ordered his troops to occupy neutral Norway. The aim of the operation was to secure territories in northern Europe that Germany could use, like those in the east, for supplies. The Norwegian operation required the mobilization of 200,000 men, 1000 planes and Germany's entire fleet. Great Britain, which had planned an analogous landing, did not stand idle. Though beaten to the punch, the British fleet counterattacked and, in front of the ports of Trondheim and

Narvik, sank ten German torpedo-boat destroyers. Nonetheless, the British attack was fended off. The Danes did not even pose the kind of tough resistance put up by the Norwegians against the Wehrmacht. Denmark was occupied on April 9, 1940 and, in order to avoid spilling blood uselessly, King Christian signed an act of surrender in which he placed the country "under the protection of Germany."

On May 10, the Chamberlain government fell in London and Winston Churchill was appointed prime minister. From the first words of his opening speech, the world understood that the war would be a long one, with no holds barred, so Hitler decided to act without further delay. The Maginot Line, which protected France from German aggression, ended at the Belgian border. This was because the strategists in Paris considered the hills and forests of the Ardennes to be impassable to an army, as there were no roads. But it was from there that the German attack came, having been planned down to the smallest detail by Erich von Manstein. With a lightning military attack Germany occupied the Netherlands and Belgium first (1000 killed and 25,000 houses destroyed during a bombing raid on Rotterdam alone). Then the attack from the Ardennes was unleashed, in which motorized teams of sappers cleared the way for the panzers under General Heinz Guderian. The Germans advanced unchallenged across France as far as the English Channel, trapping the British Expeditionary Force in a bay and the French forces in Flanders along the Belgian border. Attacked by Guderian's tanks from the south and by the might of the Wehrmacht from Belgium, the Allied army could only retreat to the Norman beach of Dunkirk and withdraw to Great Britain. The colossal rescue operation required 2500 boats and lasted from May 28 to June 5. Though it succeeded in saving the lives of 340,000 British and French soldiers, the Germans captured 500,000 French and 50,000 British troops.

Hitler with his two main advisers during the rapid French campaign: the Reichsführer-SS *Heinrich Himmler (left), and the* Parteikanzler *and the Führer's personal secretary, Martin Bormann (right).*

At this point, the road to Paris and the annihilation of France was open to the Germans. Their army broke through the enemy lines on the Somme and Marne, taking Paris on June 14, 1940. On June 10, with France on its knees, Italy entered the war on the side of the Germans *"pour nous poignarder dans le dos"* ("to stab us in the back"), as the French Prime Minister Paul Reynaud broadcast on the radio. On June 16, Reynaud was succeeded by Marshal Philippe Pétain, a WWI hero. After transferring his government – which now ruled only in southern France – to the small town of Vichy (after which the French republicwas named), Pétain signed the armistice of June 22 in the forest of Compiègne, in the same railway car – which had been turned into a museum – in which the German generals had signed the defeat of Germany on November 11, 1918.

Pétain's surrender had two dramatic consequences: open

French rebellion, proclaimed in London by General Charles De Gaulle, who committed himself to continuing the war with his men against Germany and Italy, and the cold-blooded massacre of 1500 French sailors by the British, with the sinking of dozens of ships in the Algerian port of Mers-el-Kebir, an event that led many people in France to side openly with Hitler.

Hitler's plan was to invade Great Britain in Operation *See Löwe* (Sea Lion), with a series of landings on the English coasts. To prepare the operation and weaken British morale, the Germans decided first to raise an air offensive on the coast and main cities of Britain, but something went wrong. Thanks to radar, the British were able to anticipate the arrival of the German planes and send up very strong and determined squadrons of fighters. In addition, the people on the ground reacted in a manner exactly the opposite of that forecast by the German High Command psychologists. Not only did the carpet-bombing of their cities fail to wear down the resolve of the British, it actually prompted them to an extraordinary degree of resistance. One example was the Home Guard, a force of volunteers that in a few weeks numbered a million members between the ages of 17 and 65. Immediately informed of this, Hitler gave up on the idea of an invasion and preferred to continue with air raids. Churchill responded. On November 13, 1940, the day of the official visit of the Soviet Minister of Foreign Affairs, Vyacheslav Molotov, a British air fleet rained bombs down on Berlin, destroying thousands of houses and killing thousands of inhabitants under the rubble; Molotov himself barely escaped with his life. This marked the beginning of a pitiless war of extermination of the respective civilian populations, including the destruction of Coventry by the Germans and of Dresden by the British (200,000 dead in a single night, mostly injured soldiers who had returned from the Russian front).

For nearly a year the war was fought in the skies, but it was mostly civilians who paid the price. It was at the end of this strange and dramatic year that Hitler's heir apparent, Rudolf Hess, who had been at the Führer's side from his days in Munich and had become the head of the Nazi Party, took a Messerschmitt 110 and flew alone to Scotland, where he parachuted onto the grounds of the estate of the Duke of Hamilton, with whom he was on good terms. "The Führer does not want to defeat Britain," he said, first to the duke and then to the officers sent to interrogate him. He said that Germany would respect the British Empire in return for Germany being allowed a free hand in Europe. Naturally, his claim was not taken seriously by Churchill and was immediately denied by Hitler, who considered his former deputy insane. As an indication of his personal belief, Hitler ordered the arrest of the aircraft manufacturer, Willy Messerschmitt, and Hess' entire staff of collaborators.

The truth of the situation will never be known. Hess took it with him to the grave after spending forty years in Spandau prison. Was it the act of a leader who felt sidelined and was envious of Goering, Goebbels and the other high-ranking Nazi officers (the explanation offered by William Shirer)? Or was it a trial balloon sent up with Hitler's blessing, in the hope of making peace with the British so that the Germans could attack the Soviet Union unmolested?

The attack on the Soviets began on the night of June 21, 1941, with 152 German divisions divided into three army groups. Most of the Red Army had been deployed in Siberia, fearing an attack from Japan. As a result, the Germans were able to capture 40

The German soldiers taken prisoner by the Russians after General von ▶ Paulus' surrender at the Battle of Stalingrad, which began on September 13, 1942 and ended more than four months later with the defeat of the 6th German Army.

Soviet divisions, 330,000 prisoners and a huge amount of booty in the early days of Operation Barbarossa.

So far, the Führer had not made any military blunders and his forecasts had been completely accurate, but in the summer of 1941 the Supreme Commander committed the first of his strategic mistakes. When the Central Armed Group was in sight of Moscow, he stopped its advance and directed it towards the Ukraine to support the South Armed Group, with the aim of taking the Donetz basin as quickly as possible, as it supplied oil to the Red Army. Thus, the immediate goal of the offensive was no longer Moscow (whose capture would have had an immense psychological impact), but Kiev.

The North Armed Group had also started to be worn down when, on September 15, 1940, it began a siege of Leningrad that was to last three years. And this was the second error of the great but amateur strategist, who, thinking like an ideologist rather than a soldier, wanted to punish the inhabitants of a city named after the founder of Bolshevism. He wanted them to die slowly of hunger and deprivation, rather than launching a bloody but quick and decisive battle. The Führer's wishes were granted. By the time the city surrendered 900 days after the beginning of the siege, more than 600,000 inhabitants had died of cold or hunger, but at the same time, more than one million German soldiers had remained immobilized on the front, continually looking over their shoulders to deal with the repeated, bloody attacks made on them by the Red Army.

The offensive against Moscow, which was postponed in favor of the attacks on Kiev and Leningrad, was finally ordered on October 12, 1941. However, it was too late to avoid the arrival of another adversary on the battlefield, in support of Moscow's defenders. And had Hitler been more familiar with history or studied the campaigns of Charles XII of Sweden and Napoleon, he would have realized that it was the most fearful adversary of all: winter. Throughout the winter of 1941 and the spring of 1942, the German troops remained paralyzed in front of Moscow, inflicting and suffering useless losses, while their faith in inevitable victory, which the soldiers of the Third Reich had believed in until then, began to waver.

In the meantime, following the Japanese attack on Pearl Harbor on December 7, 1941, the United States had also entered the war. All winter long, the U.S. sent huge amounts of provisions, weapons and technology to the Soviet Union, shipping them across Alaska and Siberia. Once again, the ideological fixation of the Führer frustrated his military strategy. Rather than concentrate on taking the capital, Hitler became obsessed with Stalingrad, a city that had no strategic importance but that, like Leningrad, had the audacity to bear an odious name. The Sixth Army commanded by General Friedrich von Paulus was sacrificed on the altar of Stalingrad: 250,000 Germans found themselves trapped there after more than two months of almost house-to-house and man-to-man fighting, amidst the ruins of a ghost town shelled incessantly by the 5000 cannons that ringed the city under the command of Soviet General Zukov. After witnessing the slaughter of his troops, Paulus disobeyed the order of the Führer (who had appointed him Field Marshal), surrendered to the Soviets and passed ideologically over to their side. It was February 1, 1943.

Germany had lost 140,000 men in the Battle of Stalingrad, which marked Hitler's second great defeat after the one suffered by the 'Desert Fox', General Erwin Rommel, at the hands of British General Harold Alexander at El Alamein, North Africa in September 1942.

Events snowballed after the Stalingrad catastrophe. Emboldened by its victory, the Red Army launched a dramatic counteroffensive that led to the liberation of Kiev and Leningrad, followed by the occupation of Romania, Galicia, Poland and Czechoslovakia before an advance on Vienna and then Berlin. And following the collapse of Italy, a second front opened in southern Europe. Having bombarded Rome, British and American troops had landed in Sicily on July 12, 1943, and drove the Germans up the peninsula. This led to the fall of Fascism and the arrest of Mussolini by order of the Italian king, Victor Emmanuel III. Following the liberation of the Duce by German parachutists under General Student and the armistice between the new Italian government and the Allies, Italy was divided in two. The south under the king was occupied by the Allies, while the north, where Mussolini had set up the Italian Social Republic, was under German control.

The war in Italy diverted large numbers of German soldiers from the main Russian front, but the worst was yet to come. On June 6, 1944, the largest maritime operation in history began when Allied troops landed in Normandy. Starting at dawn on D-Day, and throughout the five days that followed, 5000 ships landed 620,000 men and 220,000 tons of ordnance (a total of 95,000 trucks, tanks, cannons, cars and motorcycles). On some beaches, such as Omaha Beach, which was surrounded by German batteries, the operation turned into a massacre. Nonetheless, aided by the third of Hitler's tactical mistakes, by and large the advance of the Allies soon became unstoppable. The Führer had been convinced that the invasion would take place in Calais and on June 6, when information of the landings reached him, he still believed that the Norman operation was a bluff and opposed the use of the reserve troops against the bridgeheads being created in Normandy. By the time he realized he had been mistaken, it was too late. The advance troops under American General George Patton were already heading towards Paris.

On August 15, a second wave of Allied troops landed on the beaches of Provence in southern France and quickly advanced northwards. Lyons was occupied on August 20 and Marseilles the next day. On August 25, General De Gaulle marched into Paris, Brussels was liberated on September 3, and on September 11 the Allied forces reached the German border, where they were brought to a halt by the strenuous resistance offered by the defending German troops, even though they were fewer in number. Germany now had to fight on four fronts: Russia, Italy, France and the Balkans, though in the latter they were supported by the Chetnik Serbs led by General Mihailovich and the Croatian Ustashe.

The winter of 1944-45 was unquestionably the worst in the history of the Reich although, in December 1944, it seemed as though the tide might turn in Germany's favor in the west. Operation *Greif* had been planned by the OKW strategists in the hope of repeating the miracle of 1940 when the German troops broke through the Ardennes and conquered French territory. This time the Germans were in the minority, but they obeyed the imperative to defend the endangered fatherland. The first phase of the operation went magnificently and the entire Allied formation was forced to retreat after a series of bloody attacks by the German armored troops. This operation went down in history as the Führer's 'backlash' and it appeared to be leading to an unexpected conclusion. The Allied front had retreated over sixty miles and the more optimistic in Berlin thought that the invaders might well be chased back to the sea. But after a month of victories, the Germans were halted at Bastogne and, from January 20, General Patton recommenced his inexorable advance on Berlin at the head of his armored units. The race had begun between the Russians and Anglo-Americans to arrive first at the heart of the Third Reich.

A special place in this panorama of WWII is dedicated 'Hitler's secret weapons'. The Führer entrusted the task of reversing the course of the war, especially after the Stalingrad debacle, to a team of young scientists who initially worked at the Raketenflugplatz of Reinickendorf and then at Peenemünde, on the island of Usedom in the Bay of Pomerania. The most active person in the group was Wernher von Braun, the scientist who after the war carried out his research in the United States and sent the first man to the Moon. Von Braun was the son of the former Minister of Agriculture of the last Weimar government under Von Papen and had never shown any particular interest in weapons. In fact, since he was a youngster he had dreamed of conquering space, but in order to continue his studies he had been obliged to accept financial support from the Ministry of War since he was now director of the Heeresversuchstelle, the Army Research Center. On the evening of October 3, 1942, the staff, which took orders from General Walther Dornberger, succeeded in launching the first A4 (Aggregat 4) rocket. It was 50 feet long, 6 feet maximum in diameter, weighed over 14 tons, was propelled by liquid oxygen and alcohol and went for 125 miles at a speed of 3600 mph, reaching an altitude of more than 50 miles. A few days later an airplane took Von Braun and Dornberger to Rastenburg, in eastern Prussia, where Hitler had set up his headquarters, the Wolfsschanze or 'Wolf's Lair'. The Supreme Commander looked at the film shot at Peenemüde on October 3 over and over again, his eyes overflowing with excitement. "If we had had this rocket in 1939," he suddenly shouted, "we would not still be here making war!" Von Braun, who had just turned 30, described the various sequences of the film one by one. The legend of the secret weapons, which kept hope alive in the Axis armies until the final collapse, was born that day in Rastenburg, where Von Braun was decorated with the Iron Cross and received the title of emeritus professor. However, the most significant statement Hitler made was directed at Dornberger:

"I have had to apologize only to two men in my whole life. The first was Field Marshal von Brauchitisch. I did not listen to him when he told me again and again how important your research was. The second man is yourself. I never believed that your work would be successful. I didn't believe in rockets; now I do."

Von Braun and Dornberger were well aware that the A4 would not be able to change the course of the war: continuously sending a ton of explosives barely 186 miles distance would not destroy the Allies' front. But it was Dornberger's duty to accelerate the construction of this new fleet of rockets, especially in view of the fact that the attempts made by Goering's Luftwaffe with the 'flying bomb' (also known as V-1, from the word *Vergelt ungswaffe* or 'weapon of revenge') had not been successful.

But on October 17, 1943 hundreds of English bombers attacked the secret base of Peenemüde – which was discovered by chance by the Allies and then confirmed by a series of aerial photographs, while it was not clear what exactly the Germans were building on this island in the North Sea – causing much damage and killing 735 persons. Von Braun and Dornberger risked their lives several times to save the most important documents and drawings during the bombing. In that same period Norwegian resistance fighters led by British intelligence agents managed to destroy the 'heavy water' plant in Norway installed by another group of German scientists whose objective was the creation of the atomic bomb – just like their colleagues, who were also German, such as Einstein and Oppenheimer, who were working in the United States, where they had fled from anti-Semitic persecution.

Work on the ballistic missile proceeded in the new base, a former underground warehouse in the city of Nordhausen in Thuringia. The first 'super weapon', christened V2 by the Minister of Propaganda, took off from a ramp hidden in the Wassenaar forest near The Hague. This was a mobile ramp that was moved continuously by means of huge trucks in order to evade the Allied bombers. The target was London, where the missiles caused great damage and killed 2755 persons but did not block the huge and continuous flow of materiel and soldiers from the coast of Great Britain to the European continent. Since the main Allied landing point was Antwerp in Belgium, it was the main target of the V2s, more than 1600 of which destroyed this city. But by then the Allied invasion was inexorable.

On March 23, 1945, Hitler, by then resigned to defeat, gave the order to destroy the Nordhausen base so that the documents and infrastructure there would not fall into the hands of the enemy. But obeying this order would have meant the end of the dream of going to the Moon, so Von Braun asked two trustworthy attendants to gather and hide everything that would be useful for future research. They frantically managed to do so, escaping the notice of the SS. The entire staff was transferred to a base in Bavaria at Oberammergau, where it was taken into custody by the American Army. Under the responsibility of the U.S. Army, on September 29, 1945 Von Braun disembarked at the Fort Banks harbor in Massachussetts without a passport and under a false name. Before his arrival hundreds of pounds of papers and documents that had been stashed before the escape from Nordhausen, had already arrived in the United States. This material allowed Von Braun to continue his research and to see the *Apollo 11* spaceship – the direct descendant of the V2 – land on the Moon on July 21, 1969 with the astronauts Neil Armstrong, Edwin Alrdin and Michael Collins.

*A V-2 rocket (*Vergeltungswaffe *or weapon of revenge) on a launching pad in Holland. The first V2 attack on London killed 2755 persons. It had been prepared by a team of experts and technicians headed by Wernher von Braun, the scientist who would send the first man to the Moon in 1969.*

CHAPTER 10

THE HOLOCAUST

1933. The official anti-Semitic campaign begins. Two Nazis outside a shop owned by a Jew holding signs: "Germans! Look after yourselves! Don't buy from Jews!"

The origins of Nazi anti-Semitism can be traced to *Die Grundlagen des neunzehenten Jahrunderts* (The Foundations of the Nineteenth Century). This racist book was written and published in Germany in 1899 by a Briton, Houston Stewart Chamberlain, the son-in-law of Richard Wagner who became a German citizen in 1917, convinced – erroneously – that the Central Powers were winning WWI. Kaiser William II was enthusiastic about the work and made it required reading for all future teachers in the Reich. This decision made Chamberlain extremely popular among the supporters of Pan-Germanism and it spread anti-Jewish sentiment among their ranks.

Philosophy professor Alfred Rosenberg was enthralled by it and, using it as a source of inspiration, in 1930 he published *Der Mythus des 20. Jahrhunderts* (The Myth of the 20th Century), a book that earned him praise and admiration and ultimately led him to the gallows in Nuremberg. Hitler also read the book, and everything suddenly became clear to him. The main enemy of the German race was the Jew, because he blended in and masked himself. The Jew was like a bacillus ("like the Koch bacillus," according to the Bulletin of the Order of Physicians after the Nazis rose to power). His instruments were the press, cinema, art and literature.

But the true novelty of Chamberlain's 'ideas' lay in the criterion for recognizing Jews. According to him, the one adopted until then was wrong. Jews were not to be distinguished by their somatic features (hair and eye color, shape of the nose, etc.), but by a highly specific ethical and psychological mindset. It was not a question of stock, but a mental-spiritual issue. And yet, how could one recognize a Jew if he happened to be tall, slender, blond and blue-eyed, and had a perfect nose? The dilemma took a practical turn with the law of April 7, 1933, called the Law for the Restoration of the Civil Service. This was the first of over 400 decrees that gradually excluded Jews from the military; deprived them of their citizenship; and divested them of the right to practice first medicine, then teaching and journalism, as well as the right to receive unemployment benefits, etc. 'Civil Service Restoration' meant driving Jews from all public positions. And here arose the first paradox: what was the definition of a Jew?

Consequently, the religious criterion, which had been set aside with the publication of Chamberlain's pamphlet, was brought up again. Based on the law of February 7, 1933, in fact, if just one of a person's four grandparents were "of Jewish faith" he was considered a Jew. Even so-called civil-rights jurists within the Nazi movement protested: why should one-fourth Jewish blood prevail over three-fourths Aryan blood? Thus, a third 'race' was taken into consideration, the *Mischlinge*, 'half-breeds' of mixed Aryan and Jewish blood.

This was the 'racial novelty' of the Nuremberg Laws passed on September 15, 1935, which deprived Jews of German citizenship and prohibited mixed marriages. Regardless of the religion one professed, he/she was considered a Jew if at least three grandparents were Jewish. However, if a person also professed the Jewish faith, then two Jewish grandparents sufficed. If one had two Jewish grandparents but had repudiated the religion of one's forefathers, then the distinction went through one's spouse or companion. A person was thus considered Jewish if his/her spouse or companion was Jewish. If Catholic, then the person was considered *Mischlinge*.

There followed a series of absurd clauses, each of which drew a distinction between Jew and *Mischlinge*. An example is the following preposterous question: was a child born after July 31, 1936 (the term for a pregnancy that began after the publication of the Nuremberg Laws in the Official Reich Gazette of November 15, 1935) from an extramarital relationship between an 'Aryan' Protestant woman and a man who was Catholic but had three Jewish grandparents to be considered Jewish, *Mischlinge* or something else entirely? The answer was that the child was Jewish because both parents were guilty of 'Jewishness' – the father because he was Jewish to all effects and the mother because she was a 'whore'. An actual case in point regarded a young woman who had been caught by the SA as she was kissing her Jewish boyfriend. She was dragged around the city with a sign hung around her neck, bearing the ditty: "*Ich bin am Ort / das grösste Schwein / und lass mir nur / mit Juden ein*" (I'm the biggest whore in town / and only with Jews lie down).

In addition to all this, there was the typically German fastidiousness in further subdividing the *Mischlinge* into first- and second-degree half-castes. A first-degree half-caste had two Jewish grandparents but had abjured the faith as of September 15, 1935 and become a Christian. The second-degree half-caste had only one Jewish grandparent and was thus subject to fewer restrictions. For example, he could join the military. In short, he could die for the Führer. The tragic case of twins with two Jewish grandparents is telling. One of the young men was engaged to a Jewish girl while the other was not. The first one died in Buchenwald, but the other one – *Mischlinge* – was a hero of the Battle of Stalingrad.

In effect, it is difficult to find a rationale for the most irrational phenomenon in the world, anti-Semitism. It can probably be traced back to two circumstances or traditions. The first is the conviction held by many Christians, and cultivated for centuries even by illustrious philosophers and theologians, that the entire Jewish people is to be considered guilty of 'deicide' for having wanted Jesus condemned to death on the cross. The second stems from a stereotype according to which the Jews throughout the world resisted all attempts to have them assimilated into the traditions and cultures of their 'host' countries.

Historically, it has always been the case that a people with a strong tradition and culture has physically disappeared after being defeated militarily or after having suffered enemy occupation: the Sumerians, Celts, Phoenicians and Maya are cases in point. However, the Jews, after being defeated and dispersed by the Romans, fled to different areas of the globe (the Diaspora) yet managed to keep their customs, eating habits, traditions and faith intact, and they overcame persecution by literally making a virtue of necessity. In so doing they aroused admiration, as well as anger and vexation.

Obliged to live in ghettoes, they built synagogues there. Prevented from practicing the 'superior' trades and professions (agriculture, medicine, teaching, diplomacy and the military), they turned to money lending and the profit made through interest. This did not derive from a sort of atavistic inclination to usury – which was condemned as a sin against God and against society – as is often ignorantly claimed, but because it was the only means of survival open to them.

"The worldly God of the Jews is money," wrote Karl Marx

in 1843, though he too was Jewish – but he was married to a rich German woman from a noble family. Seven years later, Richard Wagner wrote a satirical pamphlet with the eloquent title *Das Judentum in der Musik* (Jewishness in Music), in which he claimed, "The most critical thing is to free ourselves from Jewish oppression." A short while before, all the press of Europe had blown up and manipulated one of those stories that have always been the 'joy' of journalism, a mixture of blood, fanaticism, cruelty and exoticism. A Franciscan monk and his servant had been kidnapped and killed in Damascus (then under the dominion of Egypt, a country that was very fashionable in Europe in the nineteenth and early twentieth centuries). Who had committed the crime? The foreign correspondents wrote that it was the Jews, who did so in order to procure Christian blood to make the unleavened bread for their Passover celebrations. This was yet another airing – with all the right ingredients to mobilize public opinion, governments and ambassadors – of the most wicked and idiotic myth that had weighed on the Jews for almost 2000 years, according to which every Easter the Jewish community would kidnap a Christian, preferably a child, and perform a ritual sacrifice, slashing his throat and collecting his blood in a bowl. The Christian as a lamb, a lamb like Christ.

Such diabolical legends concerning Jews – their supposed preparation of unleavened bread with human blood, ritual sacrifices and poisoning of wells – became the bread and butter of the revived anti-Semitism in Germany in the late 19th century, which was much cruder – but not more hard-hearted – than that practiced in France. This was just what inveterate anti-Semites wanted, as is demonstrated by the 1879 essay by Wilhelm Marr, the first of many increasingly repulsive books that eventually led to Adolf Hitler's *Mein Kampf*.

Marr's work, *Der Sieg des Judentums über des Germanentums* (The Victory of Judaism over Germanism), was published in 1879 and went through twelve editions in a year. Following up on this success, Marr entered politics and founded the Anti-Semitic League, thereby giving further proof of his ignorance, as the academic meaning of the word 'Semitic' had always been used to refer to the family of languages that included Arabic, as distinct from the Aryan, or Indo-European, family. Due to the success of a popular pamphlet, two innocuous adjectives (Semitic and Aryan) became the yardstick for measuring 'racial' difference, a difference that was to lead to death.

Marr not only influenced the students who were fanatical about the *Mensuren* (academic duels whose aim was to cut the opponent) but also the police force, many magistrates and even politicians. Triggered by absurd denunciations and furthered by slapdash or prejudiced police investigations, a series of trials in Germany and the Austro-Hungarian Empire (especially in Hungary, where more than 1 million Jews lived, as well as in the highly civilized Vienna and in Germany) led to the punishment of Jews of both sexes who were accused of the most incredible crimes. To all intents and purposes, Jews were being equated with those who, centuries earlier, had been persecuted because they were considered responsible for spreading the plague.

As regards the world of politics, the Christian Socialist Party (headed in Austro-Hungary for 15 years, until 1910, by the Viennese mayor Karl Lüger, who was unconditionally admired by Hitler) was anti-Semitic to the point of asking the government to drive Jews legally out of teaching and public appointments. In 1893, an *Antisemitischen Volkspartei* (Anti-Semitic People's Party) was founded in Germany and it won 16 seats in the Reichstag, the German Parliament.

Mass anti-Semitism (in the altered meaning of the word)

received another strong boost in the German world from Werner Sombart's books *Die Juden und das Wirtschaftsleben* (Jews and Economic Life, 1911) and *Die Zukunft der Juden* (The Future of the Jews, 1912). Sombart argued that the entire life of the German nation was seriously harmed by Jewish hegemony, beginning with the stock exchange and the financial publications that set stock trends. The figures seemingly supported him: in 1908, out of a total population of 200 German millionaires, 55 were Jews. Was it a plot or were they simply accomplished individuals?

The tragedy of the Jews in Nazi Germany and, subsequently, in the countries occupied by the Wehrmacht (the Third Reich army), was almost Wagnerian in its crescendo (as we have seen, Wagner was a rabid anti-Semite). At first, the tone was one of disdain. The monarchic Nationalists, the Freikorps, insulted Weimar by calling it the *Judenrepublik* (Jewish republic). The insult had a double edge: to a Prussian Junker, Jews were the lowest of the low, but in Germany in the 1920s these 'inferior' people were preeminent in politics, the press, the figurative arts and literature. For example, the following figures were Jewish: Karl Liebknecht, Rosa Luxemburg and the Bavarian Kurt Eisner, as well as the powerful foreign minister, millionaire, philosopher and writer Walter Rathenau, who was assassinated in 1922 by Nationalist extremists.

Hitler's anti-Semitism was more provincial, as befitted an Austrian, and the influence of the above-mentioned Karl Lüger was clear. For Hitler, as for Lüger, interbreeding of the races was a dreadful transgression and interbreeding with a Jew even more so. The Austro-Hungarian Empire had fallen for this reason. What did it matter if 100,000 Austrian and German soldiers of the Jewish 'race' had fought during WWI, and that 12,000 of them had died?

Jews remained the "parasites of the peoples." They exploited the hard work of others and did not create but destroyed – a belief that clashed with the fact that Arnold Schoenberg and Joseph Roth, giants of Austrian music and literature respectively, were both Jewish. Furthermore, it was thought that Jews were deceiving the world by camouflaging themselves as followers of a religion, whereas Judaism was not a religion but a people, a race. Consequently, it was a mistake to think that a Jewish German was the same as a Protestant or Catholic German, or that a Jewish Italian was the same as a Catholic or Waldensian Italian. A Jew was a Jew, and that was that.

The following extract is from Volume 2, Chapter 13 of *Mein Kampf:* "Once more the National Socialist movement has a tremendous task before it. It must incessantly remind our people.... who the true enemy of the modern world is. Rather than hate other Aryans, with whom we may disagree about everything, but to whom we are united by common blood and culture in general, we must devote ourselves to stirring indignation against the evil enemy of humanity, the true source of all our sufferings. National Socialism must act so that our deadly enemy is brought to recognition, at least in our own country.... so that the struggle against him can show other peoples the way to save Aryan humanity." Extreme anti-Semitic incitements like this literally fill the entire book, a copy of which could be found in nearly all German homes from the early 1930s on, where it was read like a sort of lay gospel.

And as we have seen in Chapter 5, Hitler wrote the following in Chapter 15 of the second volume of *Mein Kampf:* "At the beginning or even during the war, if twelve or fifteen thousand of those Marxist Jews who were corrupting the people had died from poison gas, just as hundreds of thousands of our best Germans from all social classes and professions had to face it in the field, then millions of victims would not have perished in vain on the front. If twelve thousand of these Jewish scoundrels had been eliminated in time, this probably would have saved the lives of a million Germans who would have been of value for the future." It does not seem an exaggeration to infer that Hitler was already thinking of poison gas as the most suitable method for the "final solution of the Jewish question."

The Weimar Republic fell apart in the four elections held between 1928 and 1932. Hitler's party, the NSDAP, leapt from 2.6% to 37.4% of the vote in July 1932. This proportion was slightly scaled back in November 1932, but the Nazis were still the majority party. When, on January 30, 1933, President Hindenburg asked Hitler to form a government, the new Chancellor could have been accused of anything except veiling his ideas and policies. While he was in the Landsberg fortress, where he was imprisoned after the failure of the Beer Hall Putsch on the evening of November 8, 1924, he conceived the notion of the Volkswagen, planned the highway system and wrote *Mein Kampf,* a bible of anti-Semitic hatred, which was aptly described by the Italian writer and journalist Massimo Zamorani as "the timetable of World War Two."

Although the Nuremberg Laws referred to the Jewish religion, in reality being a Jew in Germany was no longer a religious status that one could forswear by 'converting'. It had become an identifying mark that could be evaded only by fleeing the country (which the more fortunate did) or by death. Six months after the law of April 7, 1933 (Restoration of the Professional Civil Service), of the 525,000 Jews present in Germany, only 30,000 emigrated. Most of them went to the United States and Canada, some to France and Italy. Another 25,000 left the country before the Nuremberg Laws came into force, but after that it became more difficult for a Jew to emigrate. "The best Jew is a dead Jew," Goebbels shouted on the radio. The self-evident goal was a Germany free of all Jews. In September 1936, a year after the racial laws went into effect, Julius Streicher announced in his newspaper *Der Stürmer* that "the only solution is a bloody one."

On March 20, 1933, less than two months after the formation of the Nazi government, without even waiting for the law on plenary powers (which was approved three days later), the Interior Minister issued a decree to open the first concentration camp (*Lager*) at Dachau, a suburb of Munich, and he ordered 5000 political prisoners, prevalently Communists, to be transferred there from all over the country. Their heads were shaved, they were obliged to wear a uniform with vertical stripes and they had to observe a military type of discipline. Every morning, they were required to take 're-education courses', and in the afternoon they performed manual labor. The Nazi regime was not at all embarrassed. On the contrary, it liked to show it off, even organizing visits for foreign journalists. After all, it's always better to live outdoors than in a prison.

But things soon changed. In 1935 the camp was handed over to the Gestapo, which shortly afterward opened other camps at Oranienburg, Sachsenhausen and Buchenwald. The Flossenburg camp was built in 1938, Mauthausen-Gusen, Ravensbrück and Stutthof in 1939, Bergen-Belsen in 1940 and Gross-Rosen in 1941. In the meantime, the camp inmates also changed. In addition to political prisoners, who wore a red triangle on their caps, there were now common offenders (green triangle), homosexuals (pink triangle), Jehovah's Witnesses (purple triangle) and 'antisocial' persons (black triangle). And of course Jews, who were the majority of the prisoners. Their triangle was yellow, the color of those infected with the plague in the Middle Ages. With the annexation of Austria (the

Anschluss) in March 1938, another 185,000 Jews became part of the Third Reich. Within a few months it was the turn of the Jews of the Sudetenland, then those in Prague, and lastly the 2 million in Poland.

The purpose of the *Reichskristallnacht* (Night of Crystal or Night of Broken Glass), the first pogrom of the contemporary era in Germany, was to make the Jews understand what lay in store for them. Meticulously organized by the SS, the party's armed bodyguards, the storm swept over synagogues and shops owned by Jews on the night of November 9, 1938. The pretext was the killing in Paris of a German diplomat by a young German-Polish refugee. No fewer than 20,000 Nazis took part, all dressed in civilian clothes. Although the written order was to "prevent murders," the next morning 36 bodies lay on the streets of the main German cities. The shops that were destroyed numbered 7500; 191 synagogues were set on fire, 76 of which were razed.

The police did not stand idly by. A report to the government signed by the head of the *Sicherheitspoliziei* or Security Police (and future head of the Gestapo), Reinhard Heydrich, stated that "approximately 20,000 Jews were arrested, plus seven Aryans and two foreigners. The foreigners were detained to ensure their personal safety." The Jews were immediately sent to concentration camps.

Two days later, the government issued "expiatory measures" against the Jews, who were considered guilty for having sparked the *Kristallnacht* by their very presence, and Jewish communities were forced to collect an indemnity of a billion marks to be paid to the Treasury. And this was only the beginning. With a series of further decrees over the next weeks, sometimes issued just a few days apart, Jews were excluded from all health and insurance plans, and they were forbidden to go to cinemas, theaters and exhibitions or attend conferences and cultural events. Above all, it was announced that as of January 1, 1939 all shops, agencies and offices registered to Jews would be confiscated, which triggered a rush to sell property at a loss, all to the advantage of the 'Aryans'.

Could a Jew evade the prohibition of entering a cinema? Yes, but at his/her personal risk. In the period between November 12, 1938 (the day of the "expiatory measures") and September 1, 1941 (the day Jews across the country became obliged to wear the *Judenstern*, the Star of David, on their chest) repression was entrusted to the police. The Jews had a "J" stamped on their identity cards. If they were found in an off-limits place – initially forbidden to go to the cinema, theater, etc., they were subsequently banned from trains and then even public parks – they ended up in a concentration camp. It was better not to try.

Did they escape? Those with a lot of money did so quickly. Those who stayed to think it over had to decide by March 15, 1939, the day Jewish emigration was banned, after which there was no more hope. The poor (the great majority of the 375,000 Jews who were still living in Germany on July 4, 1939) were the target of an incessant, sadistic barrage of abuse and oppression. As a rule, no one helps the poor, not to speak of poor Jews. The odyssey of the steamer *Saint Louis* was a demonstration of this; in early 1939, it drifted for weeks in the Atlantic, reached the United States, but was forced to return to Europe. Even Britain, when peacetime was about to come to an end, limited the number of permits for Jews to enter Palestine, the Promised Land, which had been a British mandate since the Treaty of Versailles.

Transfers of the Jews eastwards began on October 16, 1939 shortly after the collapse of Poland. Twenty trains headed simultaneously from Berlin, Vienna, Prague and Cologne to

Lodz, each one carrying 1000 Jews. These were German families who had willingly accepted the offer to move to the ghetto in the Polish city where, they had been told, life was cheaper, it was easier to find housing and work, and there were fewer restrictions. But it was a trap. Once they reached their destination, they were forced to live approximately seven to a room, and 14,000 died in the first 18 months.

They were also told that each person could take along 100 marks, up to 110 pounds of luggage, and food for three days. Having stuffed their suitcases and bundles with as many goods and valuables as possible, bent like beasts of burden under their loads, they struggled towards the trucks that were to take them to the station. The twenty trains caused delays, jamming military railway traffic in Poland, so the SS decided that in the future the Jews would be transferred in stockcars. Freight trains might be blocked for hours and even days. It did not matter if the heat was stifling or the cold bitter.

Authorization to carry up to 110 pounds of luggage remained in force even when the transfers were no longer voluntary but obligatory and the destination was no longer a Jewish ghetto but an extermination camp. Why? The sociologist Benedikt Kautsky, a survivor of Auschwitz, explains it thus. "If the victims had known what awaited them, it would have slowed and hindered operations. This is why they were told only that they were going east to work in the Jewish ghettoes. They were advised to take as many of their personal things as possible, given that it would be impossible to procure sheets, clothes, crockery, tools and so on in those faraway places. With this plausible ruse, the Jews were tempted to take not only heaps of clothes, but also medicine, tools and especially valuables in the form of foreign currency, gold and jewelry, both openly and secretly."

In his influential book *Auschwitz*, Léon Poliakov quotes a

woman who escaped from the camp. "I was part of a group of 200 detainees destined for 'Canada'. Canada was a group of 30 huts where the objects the internees brought – generally the things they cherished – were piled together. Our work consisted of selecting the objects belonging to those who had just been gassed and incinerated. In one hut, a group chose only shoes, in another men's clothes, in a third women's clothes, in a fourth children's clothes. In another hut, called the food hut, mountains of foodstuffs, brought by those gassed when they were deported, turned moldy and rotted. Valuables were selected in another hut. A special group had to sort through the various objects taken from the condemned. I had to deal with women's clothes. They were heaped at one end of the hut and we had to make packages of 12 items, carefully folding the clothes and then tying them up. Each day dozens of trucks left to take these plundered things to Germany. We had to search through each item of clothing carefully, looking for hidden jewelry or gold."

Not all Jews believed the story of working in the east. When 523 Berlin Jews were scheduled to be transferred on April 3, 1942, 57 of them did not show up. They had committed suicide. Each transport list arrived at destination with dozens of crosses penciled in next to the names, referring not solely to those who had died during the journey, but also to those who had killed themselves. The record was reached on October 3, 1942, when 208 Jews out of 717 destined for Auschwitz (almost always entire families) preferred death. And not all Germans were ignorant of the fate that awaited the Jews. On Sunday November 11, 1941, 65-year-old Father Lichtenberg, the elderly parish priest of the Catholic church of St. Edwig in Berlin, announced from the pulpit that he wished to follow the fate of the deported Jews so he could pray with them. His wish was granted and he died in Treblinka. On July 19, 1944, Bishop

Preysing, the Cardinal of Berlin, absolved Colonel Claus von Stauffenberg who, in the confessional, announced his plan to kill the Führer.

On January 20, 1942, Reinhard Heydrich called a meeting of fifteen high-ranking Nazis in the Berlin suburb of Wannsee. Here the 'Final Solution' to the so-called Jewish question was issued: all European Jews were to be deported to the east and exterminated in gas chambers, followed by "cancellation of the proof." In other words, the bodies were to be incinerated. Among those present, Adolf Eichmann was one of the lowest-ranking officers, yet it was his duty to put the Final Solution into practice, and he was given carte blanche.

The Wannsee Conference took place in a room of a large house at 56/58 Am Grossen Wannsee. According to the minutes (later recovered and exhibited at the Nuremberg trial), "At the beginning of the meeting, the Chief of the Security Police and of the SD, SS-Obergruppenführer Heydrich, reported that the Reich Marshal had appointed him as delegate for the preparations for the final solution of the Jewish question in Europe." The minutes continued, "Able-bodied Jews, separated according to sex, will be taken in large work columns to these areas for work on roads, in the course of which doubtless a large portion will be eliminated by natural causes. Those who remain, who will undoubtedly consist of the hardiest ones, must be treated accordingly, because they are the product of natural selection and, if released, would act as the seed for a Jewish revival."

The task of carrying out the Shoah, the Jewish word for 'catastrophe', was handled by the SS, which included Allgemeine-SS (General SS), the Waffen-SS (Armed SS, which totaled 2.5 million), and the SS-Totenkopfverbände (Death's-Head Battalions) to whom responsibility for 'work' inside the camps was transferred. The SS had special rights: as soon as they had sworn an oath of loyalty, they received the dagger used, as they claimed, to wash in blood any offence to their honor. This was cited in their motto "Thy honor is thy loyalty". In 1935, Himmler issued a decree, and a sentence handed down by the Supreme Court affirmed that the "SS has the right to use arms even when the adversary can be resisted by other means."

At the end of a working day in September 1939, an SS member who was monitoring the forced labor of five Jews was feeling particularly irritated, and as a result he killed them all, one by one. A court absolved him, claiming that "his position as a member of the SS made him particularly allergic to the sight of Jews." He had even acted "impulsively, prompted by youthful recklessness." Although there was no need, Hitler signed various decrees that exempted the SS from ordinary jurisdiction and established that they would have to answer for their deeds only before the courts of the SS.

In official documents, the bureaucrats of the Third Reich never used the words 'gas chamber' and the first experiments were carried out in 1939 in Hartheim castle near Linz, Austria. These were part of a 'euthanasia program' named T4 after the address (Tiergartenstrasse, 4) of the office that was assigned to take the lives, as discreetly as possible, of 500,000 *unnütze Essern* (useless mouths) – those of unsound mind, people with Down's syndrome and sex maniacs – by means of lethal injection or gas. The death throes of the experimental subjects were filmed by the program's doctors. From the very beginning, the program was extended to all Jewish patients in hospitals. By the end of the war, 'only' 275,000 of the 'useless persons' had been done away with, just over half the intended number.

The most emblematic episode of the entire Shoah occurred in the Warsaw Ghetto. For centuries, the ghetto had been the largest Jewish enclave in the world. In September 1939, when the Polish capital fell into the hands of the Germans, 360,000 Jews and 80,000 Catholics coexisted in the ghetto without any problems. Life there comprised commercial dealings, handicrafts, banks, synagogues and a great deal of religious sentiment and activity. The ghetto was a rectangle that measured 2.5 x 1.5 miles, divided into two parts by the large road that led to Posen in one direction and Berlin in the other. It also contained lovely medieval buildings and was surrounded by a city of 1.2 million inhabitants.

The first measure effected by the occupying German forces was to oblige the *Judenrat* (Jewish Council) to take responsibility for giving homes to the Jewish families that had 'requested' to transfer east out of Germany. In less than a year, the ghetto had to accommodate 60,000 German Jews. In August 1940 work began on sealing off the ghetto, first with wooden poles and barbed wire, then with a brick wall. The Jews looked on in fear and anxiety. Nevertheless, for the moment they were still able to enter and exit the ghetto, albeit with the yellow star sewn onto their clothes.

On October 16, 1940, a decree was issued by the Governor-General, Hans Frank, that proclaimed the ghetto an 'infected zone'. The Aryans had fifteen days to leave while the 180,000 Jewish residents in other areas of Warsaw were obliged to move into the ghetto. Private dealings were permitted for the sale and purchase of property, which led to a frenzy of activity and allowed the Aryans in the ghetto to pocket at least double the market value of their houses. At the end of the period, the population density of the ghetto had risen to 5.5 people per room.

A month later, at dawn on November 15, machine-gun posts and barriers appeared at the fourteen entry points of the ghetto and from that moment on the 100,000 workers, craftsmen and professionals who worked in other parts of the city were no longer allowed to leave. And their jobs? How were they to provide for their families? This became the task (and problem) of the Jewish Council, which was obliged to distribute jobs inside the ghetto in order to foment hate, envy and animosity among the Jews. The *Ordnungsdienst* (Jewish police) was entrusted with keeping order inside the 'infected zone' and with cooling off the hotheads. The *Hausbesorger* (a sort of factory head or condominium manager) was responsible for disciplining those poor souls who were obliged to live 14 to a room in October 1941 as a result of the continuous arrival of Jews 'transferred' from Germany and the occupied territories. Chronic overcrowding led to appalling hygiene conditions and recurrent epidemics; in the summer of 1941 typhoid killed 15,700 people. The governor's office produced frighteningly precise figures for the number of calories the inhabitants of Warsaw were to receive each day: 2310 for Germans, 1790 for foreigners, 634 for Poles and 184 for Jews.

'Reduction' of the ghetto began on July 22, 1942. This entailed the deportation of ghetto residents to the extermination camps at Auschwitz, Treblinka, Majdanek and Chelmno. The operation took place in an atmosphere of extraordinary cruelty, and even the slightest reaction against the SS resulted in instant death.

Then came the Warsaw Ghetto Uprising, which was triggered by the growing atmosphere of hatred and violence, the progressive emptying of the ghetto, which provided some respite for those left behind, and above all, the knowledge that those who had to leave the ghetto faced certain extermination. The uprising began at 6 o'clock on the morning of April 19, 1943 and, to all effects, it should be considered the rebirth of the Jewish people's military capacity after two thousand years of abuse, oppression and persecution on the one hand, and division, resignation and cowardice on the other. Viewed in that context, it heralded the Jewish 'reawakening' in the world, which was to materialize later with the creation of the State of Israel and its army. In Warsaw, the Jews stopped submitting and, from that precise moment – 6 a.m. on April 19, 1943 – for every act of cruelty against the Jews there would now be a response in kind.

A few days after the rout at Stalingrad, Heinrich Himmler, the Reichsführer of the SS, ordered General Kruger, head of the SS and the Governorship's police force, to plan the final destruction of the ghetto, called the *Grossaktion*. The task was given to the tall, thin, black-haired General Jürgen Stroop, who was 48 years old. He was later captured by the Americans and handed over to the Poles, who condemned him to death and hanged him in Warsaw in 1952; the sentence was based on the daily reports he had telexed to Kruger during the 27-day *Grossaktion*.

The first of these reports, datelined 4 p.m. April 19, 1943, describes the outbreak of the revolt. Shortly after dawn, the first Nazi contingent entered the ghetto with the order to finish off the entire population, but it was halted on Zamehofa Street by a volley of Molotov cocktails, followed by hand bombs and bursts of machine-gun fire. A group of young Jews had barricaded itself in a building, flying the Polish national flag and the blue Star of David on a white background (the flag of the future Israeli army) at one of the windows. Fifteen SS soldiers were either killed or injured and two panzers were set on fire. Shortly thereafter, the building was attacked by the Germans with flamethrowers. All the young Jews died but Stroop had received his welcome. "Until today," he wrote in his second report, "we never found any difficulty in shooting down the inhabitants, but now we must face groups of 20-30 and even more Jewish criminals aged 18 to 25, including many women. The criminals defend themselves to the last man and then kill themselves rather than being taken prisoner. The women carry pistols and hand bombs hidden under their skirts."

There were still a few more surprises in store for Stroop. Some of the roads were mined and the SS trucks were blown into the air. The Germans decided to raze all the remaining 27,000 houses in the ghetto to the ground, street by street, using artillery. Another of Stroop's reports reads, "In the burning houses, the Jewish criminals throw themselves out the windows. Anyone still alive is killed on the spot by our troops." The resistance seemed indomitable. The Jewish fighters captured the weapons of the Nazi patrols they overwhelmed, escaped across roofs and fired down on their assailants. They were led by a young man of 24, Mordechai Anielewicz, the military commander of the ZOB (Jewish Combat Organization). Meanwhile, in the basements and sewer networks, women, old people and children died horribly when the Nazis poured tons of burning gasoline down the manholes.

The unequal struggle ended at 8:15 p.m. on May 16 when Stroop ordered his men to blow up the Great Synagogue and Anielewicz committed suicide so as not to fall into the hands of torturers. Stroop's last message to Governor Frank was "The Warsaw ghetto is no more." He did not like to mince words.

The following year, when 'Aryan' Warsaw was being punished for the uprising of the Armija Krajowa (the secret partisan army), Frank was the one who was chosen to handle it, due to the prowess he had shown during the destruction of the ghetto. When this revolt had been put down and the entire city destroyed, so that – in accordance with Hitler's order – nothing taller than 3 feet remained, he sent his famous telex message: "Order reigns in Warsaw."

The survivors of the Warsaw Ghetto after it was razed to the ground in May 1943 by General Stoop, who had brutally suppressed the Jewish uprising. They were taken to concentration and extermination camps.

Hans Frank had been a German lawyer who was long considered a defender of civil liberties and an opponent of the Nazi Party extremists, but he was transformed from Dr. Jekyll to Mr. Hyde shortly after being appointed Governor-General of Poland. Responsible for the elimination of Polish culture and intelligentsia, he noted in his diary on August 2, 1943: "We began with 3.5 million Jews. Only a few groups of workers remain." At Nuremberg, that entry cost him his life. He went to the gallows after asking the clerk, during the Nuremberg trial, to put the following words on record: "A thousand years will not suffice to cancel Germany's guilt for what we have done to the Jews."

THE GENERALS' REVOLT

Top *Hitler showing Mussolini, who had just arrived in Rastenburg on an official visit, the remains of the 'Wolf's Lair' after it was devastated by a bomb placed there by Claus von Stauffenberg, the leader of the assassination plot, before the July 20, 1944 meeting.*

Bottom *The Führer in a hospital a few weeks after the failed assassination. He is decorating Walter Scharff, one of the ranking officers badly wounded in the explosion, for his bravery.*

After the bloody purge of June 30, 1934 (the Night of the Long Knives), Hitler had demonstrated several times that he was prepared to eliminate anyone who stood in his way. So it was no bluff when, a few hours after the failed attempt on his life on July 20, 1944, he shouted at his generals, "I'll send the wives and children of the conspirators to the extermination camps! All traitors will die a slow death, hung from meat hooks! No military tribunals! I want a Fouquier-Tinville!"

The conspirators knew that failure would lead to these consequences, but it did not stop them from hatching a plot that began on the eve of the war and that was unsuccessful due exclusively to an incredible series of unfortunate circumstances. For years they had met, debated, formulated plans for radical political and social renewal, and sought the support of the enemy nations that called for peace but in reality wanted the destruction of Germany.

In 1942, the assassination plan was already very advanced. Those involved did not rely at all on the handful of political exiles (Communists in Russia and a few survivors in America from the days of the Weimar government), preferring to depend exclusively on their own forces to counter the Gestapo (*Geheime Staats Polizei*, the State Secret Police, which numbered 40,000 in 1944), the SS (4 million regulars), the Air Force and the Navy (completely loyal to Hitler), and the Army (the *Heer*, whose allegiance was in doubt, since the Nazi indoctrination of young officers had come to an end).

In this situation, without any outside support or the slightest hope that reasonable peace conditions might be forthcoming, the German resistance launched its attack on the Führer, who, despite the Allies' recent landing in Normandy, still had very strong domestic support. It was a case of David and Goliath.

"For a man in my situation, it is very difficult to take protective measures against an assassination attempt. I am always under threat from idealists who would willingly sacrifice their lives to achieve their aim. This is why so many attempts have succeeded in history. All in all, the best preventive measure is not to have regular habits, and to move around using a bit of imagination. In any case, I believe in the old adage that fortune favors the brave." (Adolf Hitler, *Hitler's Table Talk*, May 5, 1942).

It is clear that at that time the 'Supreme Warlord' expected an attempt on his life. He had already taken certain precautions. For instance, his cap was lined with steel and weighed about 6 pounds, under his uniform he wore body protection, and his armored cars, driven by the trusted SS, had powerful reflectors on the sides and rear to dazzle possible sharpshooters. Anyone who wanted to make an attempt on Hitler's life would also have to overcome his diabolical shrewdness and the incredible luck that seemed to protect him. The attempt made on July 20, 1944 was the last of a series that failed as a result of both factors.

The Resistance had considered a coup d'état since the eve of the invasion of Czechoslovakia. All the army generals, regardless of rank, had handed in their resignation when the Führer gave the order for 'Case Green', the plan for the attack on Prague. The idea was the brainchild of Ludwig Beck, Chief of the General Staff, who, having obtained his colleagues' agreement, had shown it to the head of the army, Field Marshal von Brauchitsch, with a memorandum containing a phrase that was to become famous: "The soldier's duty to obey ends when his knowledge, his conscience and his responsibility forbid him to carry out a certain order." Beck thought that the invasion of Czechoslovakia would spur the outbreak of another world war.

After hesitating for a month, Brauchitsch decided to visit the Obersalzberg, the Eagle's Nest, in the Bavarian Alps where Hitler had retreated to meditate, and to inform his leader of the generals' intentions. Hitler's response was an indication of the cunning of the 'Austrian corporal'. "Is that so? The generals wish to strike, do they? Very well. I'll make do without them. Or rather, I will replace them with their Chiefs of General Staff!" And so he did. At the next military conference, on August 10, 1938, he spoke for over four hours to the Chiefs of the General Staff of the various units of the Army (as is mentioned above, there was no problem with the Navy or Air Force, as the officers were all Nazi supporters) and received unconditional obedience and consensus from the young officers.

From that moment on, Ludwig Beck, who had immediately resigned his commission, began to consider a putsch. He and the most well-known opposition members – Field Marshall Erwin von Witzleben, Rome ambassador Ulrich von Hassell, Leipzig burgomaster Carl Gördeler, and Admiral Canaris – decided to arrest the Führer and haul him before a people's court as a war criminal as soon as Hitler gave the order to march on Czechoslovakia. At that time, these men did not think a war would be dangerous for Germany (military victory seemed as possible to the generals as it did to Hitler), but in their opinion the Führer was, as Beck put it, "the arch-enemy of the world." This definition implied Beck's opposition to the persecution of Jews and his repudiation of war as a solution for political problems.

The plans for the putsch were prepared. Hitler was to be arrested immediately after ordering the attack, while General Franz Halder, the new Chief of the General Staff in Beck's place, would stop the army marching south on Sudetenland. During the trial against Hitler, Beck would appeal to the German people over the radio to show that France and Great Britain would certainly have declared war as a result of their alliance with Czechoslovakia if Hitler had not been stopped at the last moment. It was the conspirators' intention to provide the people and the Nazi Party with proof, as this would be the only way to avoid a civil war.

Beck organized things quickly. Gördeler and Hassell were to constitute a provisional civil government, Witzleben would occupy Berlin militarily, install martial law and arrest the hierarchies, and General Höpner would use his panzers to hold off the diehard Nazi loyalists who would undoubtedly march on the capital from Munich.

Only one detail was missing: the support that Beck was confident he could obtain from London, the official declaration that Great Britain would declare war on Germany in the event of an attack on Czechoslovakia. And this was where the plan fell through. Beck's envoys to London – Ewald von Kleist and Theodor Kordt – were not even received. The British and French Prime Ministers, Neville Chamberlain and Édouard Daladier, betrayed the pact with Prague in order to avoid war and joyfully accepted Mussolini's invitation to the Munich Conference on September 29 "for the salvation of peace." How would it have been possible to arrest the Führer who had just won a war without firing a shot? How could they imprison the man whom all Germany was cheering? As Hans Gisevius, a witness at Nuremberg, later said, "Chamberlain had saved Hitler."

Given the impossibility of a strategic operation in grand style, the Resistance decided to change tactics to a more direct method, assassination, but each time their meticulously prepared plans to kill Hitler failed. A dozen or so 'overcoat attacks' – to be carried out by young officers who volunteered as suicide bombers, concealing explosives in their overcoats – had always been foiled by the Führer's extreme mobility. More organized attempts also failed due to unforeseen circumstances. On one occasion, a time bomb was placed on an airplane but the percussion pin did not work, and on another occasion an American bomber destroyed the conspirators' cache of time bombs.

However, the main reason for the failures can be attributed to the plotters themselves, as they lacked an iron-willed and decisive leader who would take action into his hands. Such a leader only appeared at the beginning of 1944: Count Claus Philipp Schenk von Stauffenberg, the Chief of the General Staff to the Reserve Army command with headquarters on the Bendlerstrasse in Berlin.

Thirty-seven years old, von Stauffenberg was tall, dark-haired and extremely handsome. He was a practicing Catholic and the great-grandson of Field Marshal Gneisenau (the creator of the Prussian General Staff) and a descendant of Field Marshal Yorck von Wartenburg, who defeated Napolcon at Tauroggen. An officer of the historic Bamberg Cavalry Regiment since the age of 19, his aversion to Nazism arose in 1938 at the time of the anti-Semitic pogrom. To him, the war that followed soon after seemed like the opportunity to distance himself from the crimes that so upset him. He fought in Poland, France and Russia (where he had instructed Ukrainian anti-Communist volunteers, hoping to use them "to liberate Russia from Stalin after we have liberated Germany from Hitler"). And he had been seriously wounded in North Africa, where he lost an eye, his right hand and two fingers of his left hand during the Battle of Kasserine on April 7, 1943. In September he had entered service in Berlin as a lieutenant colonel and Chief of General Staff to General Friedrich Olbricht, another active member of the Resistance.

The series of failures to kill Hitler prompted him to try personally. He practiced with a pair of pliers on what were known as 'English bombs'. These were special explosives dropped by the British to Allied secret agents to use in attacks. Instead of the noisy ticking of a clock in a time bomb, these contained a small phial of corrosive liquid that ate away a wire that held the percussion pin. Admiral Wilhelm Canaris' Abwehr (Military Secret Service) had collected several of these bombs and passed them on to the Resistance.

Through his personal authority and powers of persuasion, Stauffenberg quickly came to the fore among the other opponents to the regime, and soon Beck and Witzleben also accepted his leadership. He was not only a man of action but, being a liberal with a strong sense of Christian unity, he had clear political ideas. When he realized that the plot lacked field marshals in active service, he won over an important figure to the cause, Erwin Rommel. Now everything was ready.

In German mythology, the Valkyries were maidens charged by the gods to choose the heroes who had to die. And we can easily imagine the twinkle that must have gleamed in the eyes of Admiral Canaris, when he proposed Operation Valkyrie to Hitler, stating that it would allow the Reserve Army to maintain order in the event of a revolt by the millions of foreign workers deported to Germany. Thus, under the cover of Operation Valkyrie, officially approved by the Führer, the conspirators were able to work undisturbed and iron out their plans to occupy Berlin and other important cities once Hitler was killed.

The plan provided for the occupation, within two hours, of the radio stations in Berlin, the telegraph and telephone offices, the Reich Chancellery, and the ministries and headquarters of the SS. It also called for the arrest of Goebbels, the only minister in the capital, given that he was also the Nazi party head of the city (all the others followed Hitler around in his continual movements from one headquarters to another). Lastly, the tank corps under Krampnitz were to advance on the capital to stifle any attempted resistance by the SS.

Next, the new head of State, Beck, and the new Chancellor, Gördeler, would appeal for unity on the radio, and the new supreme commandant of the Wehrmacht, Witzleben, would request immediate armistice on the Western Front while fighting continued on the Eastern Front.

It was planned that Wilhelm Keitel, the leader of the OKW, would be killed in the explosion, so he would be unable to create obstacles by issuing orders that countered Witzleben's (but in fact the exact opposite occurred). As for the irresolute chief of the Reserve Army, Friedrich Fromm, it was planned that he would be arrested and replaced with General Erich Höpner. And as the operation could only be put into action by Fromm, orders supposedly drawn up by him and bearing his forged signature had been compiled and locked in the safe of his assistant, Olbricht, together with the declarations and appeals to be broadcast by radio and the press releases to be issued to newspapers. All this material was typed up at night by General Henning von Treschkow's wife and her friend Margarethe von Oven.

On the afternoon of July 19, 1944, Claus von Stauffenberg was in his office at the General Staff of the Reserve Army on the Bendlerstrasse when he received a telephone call ordering him to present himself at 1 p.m. the next day at Rastenburg, the Führer's headquarters, for a military meeting. He was to report on the new divisions of the *Volksgrenadiere*, more cannon fodder for the Russian front. The colonel immediately began to prepare his report. At 8 p.m. he left the office, climbed into his car and headed home. On his journey, he stopped to pray in the Catholic church in Dahlem. Ten days earlier he had confessed to the archbishop of Berlin, Cardinal Count von Preysing, that he planned to kill the Führer, and the cardinal had not attempted to place any religious obstacles in his path. The decision had been made.

The next day – whether Goering, Himmler or Bormann were present or not (the attempt had been postponed three times already due to their absence) – the bomb would go off. At ten o'clock, the small, twin-engine Heinkel plane of General Éduard Wagner, a member of the conspiracy, landed at Rastenburg. Stauffenberg and his assistant, Lieutenant Werner von Häften, got out. Waiting for them was the short, hunchbacked General Helmuth Stieff, another conspirator, whom Hitler called "the poisonous dwarf." Stieff handed Stauffenberg the bomb, which was wrapped in a shirt. It had been prepared during the night with thinner wire than usual so that it would be corroded by the acid in ten minutes.

Stauffenberg placed the bomb in his briefcase and then, followed by Häften, he went to the Wolf's Lair, where he left his assistant with General Fritz Fellgiebel, another conspirator, entered the hut of Keitel (head of the OKW), and hung up his cap and belt in the anteroom. The Field Marshal told him that the meeting had been moved up to half past noon, as the Führer was expecting Mussolini at 2:30 p.m. following the Italian leader's arrival at the Görlitz military station. The meeting was to be held in the Gästebaracke, a wooden casemate reinforced with concrete walls instead of the bunker, where the effect of the explosion would have been fatal. Nonetheless, the news did not perturb him.

It was time to go. Stauffenberg asked to be excused for a moment saying, "I've forgotten my cap and belt." This was the pretext to allow him to set the bomb timer in action. He turned back and with his remaining three fingers he opened the brief-case, unwrapped the package, took the pliers and broke the phial. The time was exactly half past noon. In ten minutes, the bomb would explode.

Annoyed, Keitel came up to Stauffenberg asking, "What the devil are you waiting for? We're already late." They hurried to the Gästebaracke. It was a room measuring 16'6" x 41', with three large windows that were open because it was a muggy day.

Adolf Hitler, two stenographers (Berger and Hagen) and twenty high-ranking officers were standing around a rectangular oak table (20' x 6'6") that stood on two large supports, one at either end. Stauffenberg sat down between General Korten and Colonel Brandt, a few paces away from Hitler, and placed his briefcase on the floor. He murmured to Brandt, "I have to go out for a moment. I'm expecting a telephone call," and left stealthily. No one noticed his departure, as everyone present was concentrated on what General Heusinger was saying about the latest break throughs by the Russians on the Eastern Front.

As Brandt moved towards the map on which the speaker was indicating a point, he tripped over the briefcase and automatical-ly picked it up and moved it against the outer side of the table's support: it was this act that saved Hitler's life and cost Brandt his own.

At 12:39 p.m. Heusinger was about to finish his report. Keitel looked around for Stauffenberg to warn him to get ready as he was due to speak next, but realized that he was not there. Irritated by the young colonel's unjustifiable behavior, he hur-ried out to call Stauffenberg. Heusinger was just saying "….if we do not manage to withdraw the troops from Lake Peipus, then a catastrophe…." when the bomb exploded. It was 12:40 p.m. exactly.

Running, Stauffenberg had managed to put about 50 yards between himself and the Gästebaracke. He was thrown to the ground by the pressure waves and saw bodies hurled through the windows and the wreckage fall to the ground with a deafening crash all around. He got up, shouted to Fellgiebel, who appeared at a doorway, to phone immediately to Berlin, and ran to the car where Häften was waiting with the engine running.

As Stauffenberg and his assistant reached the exit, the smoke inside the Gästebaracke was clearing. The uninjured Keitel groped his way towards the Führer and led him outside. Hitler's clothes and hair were burnt, his trousers ripped, his right arm partially paralyzed, his right leg seriously burned and his hearing damaged. A beam had fallen from the ceiling and scraped his back. His first words were, "Luckily there were no women present." The explosion had killed the stenographer Berger on the spot and mortally injured General Schmundt, General Korten and Colonel Brandt, all of whom died a few hours later. The others suffered various injuries. At first, the survivors assumed there had been a Russian air attack, but when they saw the hole in the floor, they thought a bomb had been hidden beneath the bricks. It was only a couple of hours later, when the roll call of the wounded was made in the field hospital, that they realized Stauffenberg was missing.

A few hours later, in the presence of Mussolini, who had arrived on his special train at 4 p.m., Hitler strode up and down the room exploding with rage and hate, foaming at the mouth. He shouted that he should have uprooted "those bastards" from the face of the earth, that he should have destroyed them and torn their wives and children to shreds. "Give me Berlin!" he screamed, "I want Goebbels on the phone!" Once he got through to his Minister of Propaganda, he ordered him to get ready, as he wanted to speak to the nation on the radio. Then, all of a sudden, he fell silent, as white-jacketed waiters entered to serve tea. The Italians were dumbstruck. Marshal Graziani suggested that they leave, so Hitler accompanied them to the station. Before the Duce got into the carriage, Hitler took his hands in both of his, looked the Italian leader in the eyes as though he were a lover, and said, "Please believe me when I say that I consider you the only friend I have in the world." Mussolini was moved and those watching did not know where to look. However, according to the memoirs written by Rahn, the German ambassador in Salò, "A minute later, when it was my turn to bid farewell to the Führer, he shot a quick and eloquent look at Mussolini's back and whispered, 'Rahn, be very careful!'"

Three hours after the explosion, at 3:30 p.m., Stauffenberg landed at the military airport of Berlin-Rangsdorf and rushed to phone Olbricht to learn, to his anger, that nothing had been done in the meantime because, as Olbricht stated to defend himself, "We did not know from Fellgiebel's call whether Hitler was dead or alive." Stauffenberg swore and ordered the vice commandant of the Reserve Army to give the green light to Operation Valkyrie immediately. It began three hours later than expected, but still in time. Major Jacob, at the head of the cadets of the Döberitz infantry school, occupied the radio station and Major Remer, commander of the Grossdeutschland Infantry Regiment, headed off to take over the ministries.

Stauffenberg rushed to the Bendlerstrasse office and immediately telegraphed orders for Operation Valkyrie to begin in foreign capitals. In Paris, General von Stülpnagel did not hesitate for an instant, and, in just half an hour, all members of the SS in the French capital were disarmed and imprisoned with their commander, SS-Gruppenführer Karl Oberg. Meanwhile, General Beck had arrived with the radio appeal to the nation in his pocket.

Chapter 11

At that moment (4:45 p.m.), General Fromm, the commandant of the Reserve Army whom no one had thought to render
harmless, managed to contact Rastenburg and, having found
out that Hitler was very much alive, began to shout that there
was treachery afoot. "Stauffenberg, come here immediately!" he
ordered. The colonel entered and the general continued, "Shoot
yourself immediately! Your assassination attempt has failed!" At
this point, the innate generosity of the noble colonel proved to
be his undoing. Fromm, who should have been killed at least four
hours before, was not only courteously declared under arrest, but
he was locked in a comfortable room with sofas, a mobile bar
and, above all, a telephone, which he used to contact as many
commandants as possible and warn them not to follow the orders
of Operation Valkyrie bearing his forged signature. The same
chivalrous treatment was given to a dozen of Fromm's close collaborators and SS-Oberführer Piffräder, who had arrived to arrest
Stauffenberg and the others.

It was then that the conspirators committed their second,
irreparable mistake. Höpner, who had replaced Fromm as the
commandant of the Reserve Army, gave a series of excited orders
by telephone and telegraph that generated confusion in the various units. First they had received orders signed by Fromm, then
from Höpner. Who should they obey? What was going on? The
result was that nothing was done.

In the meantime, Major Otto Remer, who had followed
orders exactly, went to report to General von Hase, the military
commander of Berlin, in keeping with the Operation Valkyrie
plan. This he did in record time. No resistance was offered as the
SS guards to the ministries had given way to the veterans of the
Grossdeutschland and let themselves be disarmed. Hase ordered
Remer to take twenty men to the Ministry of Propaganda, arrest
Goebbels and bring him to Hase's office. Reme clicked his heels

and left. A quarter of an hour later, he left twenty men in the anteroom and broke into Goebbel's office, holding a pistol. "Herr Reichsminister, you are under arrest!" The following dialog occurred:

"You're insane! You're forgetting your oath of loyalty to the Führer!"

"The Führer is dead, and I am freed of my oath."

"He's not dead! He's alive! And I can prove it to you!"

Nervously Goebbels pressed the button on the phone. He was passed straight to the Rastenburg headquarters. After a few seconds Hitler came on the line. Goebbels quickly explained the situation, then passed the receiver to Remer.

"Major, this is the Führer, do you recognize my voice? A group of traitors tried to kill me but I am alive and right now I need you." All the blood drained from Remer's face and he mechanically came to attention. His instructions followed: "I order you to arrest the traitors. Follow Goebbel's directives, do you understand? I will give you the Iron Cross with swords and diamonds. From this moment you are a general!"

There was nothing to add. In that instant, Remer became the nemesis of the putsch. Within two hours he had liberated the ministries, occupied the Kommandantur in Berlin, arrested Hase, surrounded the Bendlerstrasse with 300 men and machine guns, and ordered Major Jacob (who had taken the radio station) to return to the barracks, thus allowing Goebbels to notify the country of the failed assassination attempt and preventing Beck from launching his appeal to the German people.

At Bendlerstrasse, Stauffenberg heard the hoarse voice of Goebbels on the radio and decided to react by telegraphing to all army units that the minister was lying and that Hitler was really dead. He had killed the Führer himself and, therefore, they were all freed from their oath of loyalty. But half an hour later, at 7:30

p.m., Keitel used the OKW telegraph machines to tell all units to obey his orders alone. This marked the end. The coup d'état had failed.

At exactly 8 o'clock that evening, eight of Fromm's subordinates – who had been arrested with their chief but had been able to leave the Bendlerstrasse, taking guns from the Gestapo command – broke into the Ministry of War. They were commanded by two 28 year-old men, Lieutenant Colonels Franz Herber and Bodo von der Heyde. They entered Olbricht's office with their machine guns ready and came upon the conspirators, who were desperately trying to contact military units ready to collaborate. "You're all under arrest!" Heyde informed them. They all raised their hands except Stauffenberg, who tried to rush to the door. He was stopped by a bullet that passed through his arm.

Beck, Höpner, Olbricht, Olbricht's General Chief of General Colonel Mertz von Quirnheim, Stauffenberg and his assistant Häften were immediately taken to Fromm. The others were held in Olbricht's office. Fromm was standing behind the desk where they had left him, drinking, smoking and telephoning at will. He looked at them ironically. The first to speak was Beck. Calm and serene, he courteously asked to be given a pistol. Fromm did not turn a hair. He nodded to a young second lieutenant to give the weapon to the former Chief of the General Staff of the German Army. "Be quick about it, please," Fromm said icily. Beck turned towards the wall and shot himself in the temple; he fell to the floor but was still alive. From behind his desk Fromm added, "Help the old man." The second lieutenant picked up the pistol that had fallen to the ground, grabbed Beck by the armpits and dragged him into the hallway, where he finished him off with a shot to the head, as one would do with an injured horse.

Everyone was petrified. Fromm left the room to return ten minutes later. "I have ordered a court martial. The court has condemned to death, for high treason, Colonel Mertz, General Olbricht, Lieutenant Häften, and this colonel whose name I do not wish to speak," and he indicated Stauffenberg, who was ashen from loss of blood. "The sentence will be carried out as soon as you have written to your families."

Precisely at midnight, the condemned officers were shot in the courtyard of the Bendlerstrasse building, illuminated by the headlights of two trucks as Remer had them face the wall. Before being gunned down, Stauffenberg shouted, "Long live free Germany!"

The execution of the ringleaders was just the beginning.

Already on the day after the attempted assassination, the inquest was transferred to the 'Special Commission for July 20', presided over by the head of the Gestapo, Heinrich Müller, and numbering about 400 officers. Interrogations took place in Prinz-Albrechtstrasse. In just a few days the details of the plot became apparent. The huge quantity of material found in the Bendlerstrasse offices and the confessions, often extorted by means of torture, led to more than 7000 people being taken to the cells of the Gestapo and, later, to the gallows.

On the first day of the commission's existence, July 21, General Heinz Guderian, the creator of German armored vehicle formations, was appointed the new Chief of the General Staff of the Wehrmacht. Three days later, he replaced the military salute with the Nazi salute; on July 29 his order of the day included the following: "Every officer of the General Staff must be a Nazi leader." On August 4 a military 'Court of Honor' was formed, presided over by Field Marshal Karl von Runstedt (the man who had underestimated the Normandy landings and thus lost the battle of northern France) and composed of Field Marshal Keitel and three generals, Guderian, Schroth and Specht. The task of the court was to expel from the Wehrmacht all officers who had been involved in the conspiracy so that they could be judged as civilians by the Volksgerichtshof, the newly created People's Court.

Stripped of their uniforms and dressed in threadbare clothes, shoes without laces and trousers without belts, the conspirators appeared individually before the tribunal in the Berlin law courtrooms. The first of a long series of trials, which was the only one to be held in public (the others were held behind closed doors), began on August 7 and ended the next day. Sitting at the table of the defendants, who had become mere skeletons, were Field Marshal von Witzleben, Generals Höpner, Stieff and Hase, and Count Peter Yorck von Wartenburg, the leading force behind the Kreisau Circle and a direct descendant of the man who had defeated Napoleon.

The president of the People's Court, Roland Freisler, insulted the accused throughout the trial. "You filthy old man!" he shouted at Witzleben, whose false teeth had even been removed, "stop fiddling with your trousers!"

They were hanged at Plötzensee prison in a large room once used as a kitchen. Attached to the wall were eight meat hooks. The men were stripped to the waist and a noose made of piano wire or iron wire was tied around the neck of each one. Then they were hoisted onto the hooks by the SS and died a slow, agonizing death, all of which was filmed by cameramen from the Ministry of Propaganda. That day, and during the days that followed, 150,000 feet of film were recorded and presented to the Führer. Goebbels fainted as he watched it beside his leader, but Hitler gloated obscenely and ordered the films to be shown at Army training schools.

The film of the last agony and death of Erwin von Witzleben, the supreme commandant of the Wehrmacht (albeit only for a few hours), was shown to the cadets of the Berlin military school. What can only be called a miracle occurred; without having communicated with one another, all the young men rose together and left the room. After that episode, the films were destroyed.

What has remained, however, are the statements taken by the stenographers of the trials, which continued hurriedly until February 3, 1945, the date an American bomb that fell on the People's Court courtroom killed Roland Freisler, destroyed the trial files and allowed Lieutenant Fabian von Schlabrendorff, who was being tried, to avoid the death sentence, to hide until the end of the war and to write the valuable book *Offiziere gegen Hitler* (Officers against Hitler).

Orders for the capture of Carl Gördeler, the Chancellor in charge of the provisional government, had been given three days before the July plot, so he had gone into hiding. Hitler put a price of a million marks (almost 10 million dollars today) on his head. At first, relatives and friends took him in and no one betrayed him, but on the morning of August 12, ragged, hungry and exhausted – and unwilling to endanger those who were risking their lives to help him – he entered a tavern in the village of Konradswalde, where a Luftwaffe auxiliary, Helene Schwärzel, recognized him. Gördeler escaped into the nearby woods but was tracked down by SS dogs. He was hanged on February 2, 1945 with his brother Fritz, former minister Popitz and the Jesuit priest Alfred Delp.

Count Helmuth von Moltke was hanged on January 23, 1945; Adam von Trott zu Solz on August 25, 1944; Friedrich von der Schulenburg (the former ambassador to Moscow) on November 10; Ulrich von Hassell on September 8 (Hassell was the former ambassador to Rome, and his diary, published posthumously by his daughter with the title *The Other Germany* following the war, remains the most moving description of the

German Resistance); General Erich Fellgiebel on August 10; and Admiral Canaris and his assistant Colonel Hans Oster (who was responsible for hundreds of masterly spying coups during the war) on April 9, 1945. They, as well as so many others, were all executed mercilessly.

It is easier to list those who survived. In addition to Schlabrendorff, there was the lawyer Joseph Müller, nicknamed Ochensepp (Joe the Bull) due to his size, who was a friend of Pope Pius XII and was assisted and supported by the pontiff in his vain attempts to negotiate peace with the Allies; the trade union representative Jacob Kaiser; General Hans Speidel, who became the first Chief of the General Staff of the new Bundeswehr after the war; Dr. Eugen Gerstenmaier, who became president of the Bundestag in the 1960s; and a very small number of others who were of minor importance. In Berlin, the SS executed a group of 20 condemned men by machine gun on the night of April 22-23, when the Russians were practically at the gates of the city. Two of these were the brother of the minister Dietrich Bonhöffer (one of the first to be hanged) and Albrecht Haushofer, the son of the scientist who was a friend of Rudolf Hess. As soon as Haushofer's father heard the news, he committed suicide out of grief.

The last group – consisting of General Franz Halder (former Army Chief of the General Staff), Hialmar Schacht (former Minister of Economics and savior of the reichsmark) and General Alexander von Falkenhausen (with them were the former Austrian Chancellor Kurt von Schuschnigg and former French president Léon Blum) – was freed by the Americans in Niederdorff, a village in the Tyrol, just as a squad of fleeing SS was preparing to massacre them. Schuschnigg recounted the episode, which ended with the Americans killing the SS men, to the author of this book in the 1960s.

Those who had participated directly in the plot were not the only ones to be hanged; this fate also awaited hundreds of Germans who had heard of its existence but had failed to inform the Gestapo. One of these was a humble priest, Father Hermann Wehrle, who had received the confession of one of the conspirators, Major von Leonrod, shortly before the putsch. After Leonrod revealed this fact under torture, the priest was arrested, sentenced and executed. Fromm, the zealous coward, was killed on March 19 but, rather than being hanged he was shot upon orders from the Führer.

But not all of them gave Freisler – Hitler's pitiless Fouquier-Tinville – the sadistic joy of being paraded before him, crushed and silent. Beck (as described above), Baron von Freytag-Loringhoven, and Generals Éduard Wagner, Henning von Treschkow and Werner Schräder committed suicide immediately after the abortive putsch. General Karl Heinrich von Stülpnagel, the iron-willed governor with bristly hair who had had all the SS arrested in Paris, was called to appear before Hitler a few days later. On his way back to Germany, he stopped the car in a forest in Verdun where he had fought as a captain during World War I, walked into the woods and shot himself in the head. Unsuccessful, he was treated by the SS and, as soon as he recovered, was hanged on a meat hook.

The end of Field Marshall Erwin Rommel is widely known. After recovering late in the fall of 1944 from the serious wounds he had suffered during an air attack on his car, his death was decreed personally by Hitler, despite the fact that he had long been the Führer's favorite and had not been involved in the attempt on his life (he felt that murdering Hitler was a mistake, as it would make him a martyr in the eyes of the people). Rommel's name had been mentioned by an officer on the Western Front, who had been tortured by the Gestapo. The officer had claimed that Rommel had said, "Tell those in Berlin that they can count on me." This fact was secretly reported to Keitel, who informed Hitler.

Although Rommel was one of the few trusted military leaders left in the Wehrmacht, Hitler was unable to refrain from taking his revenge. On October 14, 1944, General Burgdorf and General Maisel from the Führer's headquarters visited Rommel at his home in Herrlingen, near Ulm, which had been surrounded by SS members and five tanks for several days. Burgdorf had with him a capsule of cyanide. The two guests talked with the field marshal for about a quarter of an hour, and then Rommel slowly went upstairs, entered the room of his son, fifteen-year-old Manfred (who many years later became mayor of Stuttgart) and calmly told the boy, "In fifteen minutes I will be dead. Don't be afraid for me, I have some poison that will kill me in three seconds. Don't say anything to your mother now. Take care of her afterwards."

He put on his old Afrika Korps leather jacket, took his marshal's staff and went out to the car of his two guests. Fifteen minutes later, the hospital in Ulm called to inform Frau Rommel that her husband had died of 'cerebral congestion'. Rommel was buried with full military honors at the expense of the State. Hitler sent Rommel's widow a telegram of condolence: "The name of Field Marshal Rommel will forever remain associated with the heroic battles fought for the greatness of Germany."

We cannot end this chapter on the July 20 plot without discussing the behavior of the Allies. Their indifference and deafness to the hopes of the conspirators led them to reject the desperate plea for help that Beck made to Allen Dulles, the head of the US Secret Service in Switzerland, on the eve of the putsch. The request was made by Hans Gisevius and Adam von Trott zu Solz. The two emissaries were asking for three American divisions to parachute on Berlin immediately after Hitler's death, but the two men were not even received.

Other contacts included the one between the Lutheran pastor Dietrich Bonhöffer and the Anglican Bishop of Chichester, who met in Stockholm in May 1942. On that occasion, to demonstrate the seriousness of the plot, Bonhöffer supplied the Englishman with the list of names of members of the Resistance. However, the list ended up in the hands of Radio London – no one knows how – and was broadcast, thus condemning dozens of members of the German Resistance to death.

For that matter, the way the Allied radio stations and newspapers communicated news of the plot to the world differed little from Hitler's manner. "A very small clique of ambitious, unscrupulous, criminal and stupid officers formed a plot to kill me," the Führer stated in his message to the people on July 20, adding that they would be extinguished without pity. The same night, the radio station in Washington broadcast news of the attempt, calling the plotters "a small clique of ambitious officers." Ten days later, speaking on the subject to the House of Commons, Winston Churchill stated, "The highest personalities in the German Reich are murdering one another, or trying to...."

The generals were not the only ones who opposed Hitler. After the institution of the dictatorship on March 23, 1933 (*Ermächtigungsgesetz*, the law on plenary powers or the Enabling Act), opposition grew in various areas of the public despite the regime of terror and violence, and their actions ranged from nonalignment to help offered secretly to persecuted Jews, and from mere criticism to active conspiracy. In the front line against the Nazi regime was the Catholic Church. The encyclical *Mit brennender Sorge* issued by Pope Pius XI on March 14, 1937 clearly and unmistakably condemned Nazism as a pagan and racist ideology. Shortly after the publication of the encyclical,

Catholic associations in Germany were dissolved, the editors of their magazines were arrested and often sentenced to death, dozens of ecclesiastics were arrested on false pretences (farcical trials for fraud or acts of immorality were staged against bishops and parish priests), and monasteries and ecclesiastical assets were confiscated, along the lines of the Jacobins during the French Revolution – a move copied by none other than the Communist regimes. Nonetheless, the bishop of Münster, Count von Galen, found the courage in 1941 to speak out against "racial persecution, insane euthanasia, indiscriminate arrests, and violation of the most basic human rights." Meanwhile, famous Jesuits like Father Delp and Father Rösch, the Provincial of Bavaria, became the spiritual guides of the Kreisau Circle from which Colonel Stauffenberg emerged.

The experience of the Protestant Church was different, since certain sections had supported Nazism from the outset. In July 1934 the inevitable split occurred. The Deutsche Christen national church was formed and elected Ludwig Müller as the *Reichsbischof* (Bishop of the Reich). Ministers who were not Aryan were hounded out of the church. The *Arierparagraph* (Aryan paragraph) proclaimed unconditional war against the Jews and the "holy alliance between the swastika and the cross of Christ." The Reichsbischof wrote, "We are the SS of Jesus in the struggle for the destruction of the physical, social and spiritual ills of the nation." The dissidents and those expelled reacted to this madness with a synod held in Barmen. The Bekennende Kirche or Confessional Church was formed, with ministers Martin Niemöller, Hans Asmussen and Dietrich Bonhöffer as its spiritual heads. All were to pay for their beliefs with their lives, as were Catholic priests and bishops.

One moving episode in this context concerned the White Rose student group in Munich, whose members adhered to various religions. The siblings Hans and Sophie Scholl had written letters that they copied with a duplicator and sent out to thousands of Germans accusing the Nazis of impiety and crimes. In February 1943, the Gauleiter of Bavaria, Paul Giesler, who had seen some of the White Rose letters, decided to confront the 'rebels' in their den. At the university he gave a deliberately vulgar speech in which he invited the male students to go and fight "rather than waste their time on books" and the girls "to make themselves useful, perhaps by bearing a son a year to the Third Reich." "I have no doubt", he continued, "that the prettier ones among you will find a man to mate with. For the unattractive girls, I offer my SS escort."

This was too much. The Gauleiter was whistled at and the SS kicked out of the hall. That afternoon various processions of students marched through the city streets, assaulting the SS and the police. The Scholls (Hans was a medical student of 25 and Sophie a biology student of 21) were recognized as the leaders of the protest, arrested and decapitated with an axe. They were followed by the group's moving force, Kurt Huber, a deeply Catholic professor of Theoretical Philosophy. In his last letter he wrote, "Death is the fair copy of my life."

APOCALYPSE
IN BERLIN

There was a brief period (March and April 1945) in which Hitler was convinced that there would be an imminent clash between the Allies and the USSR as the Red Army inexorably advanced westward. This conviction was supported on April 7 when the Gestapo captured three Soviet agents who had parachuted into the area near Templin. Interrogated with the usual methods of torture, the three confessed that they had been instructed to discover the "Anglo-American plans for aggression against the USSR." Stalin clearly did not trust his Western allies. For a moment Hitler thought he had erred in not having listened to Mussolini who, back in the dramatic year 1944, had exhorted him to sue for armistice in the West so that they could all tackle the Red avalanche together. However, the illusion did not last long. Of the two Allied leaders – Churchill and Roosevelt – the American was the stronger, and he would never have gone against his word to Stalin.

Though safe in his bunker at the Chancellery, Hitler and his retinue lived through the demoralizing carpet-bombing that, each night, devastated what remained of the Reich's cities. After Dresden it was the turn of Chemnitz, then Kassel, Worms,

◀ *American soldiers reading about the death of Adolf Hitler in* Stars and Stripes *on May 2, 1945, the day the Battle of Berlin ended.*

Würzburg and Duisburg. The catastrophic news (tens of thousands of civilians killed every day) arrived by radio and telegraph in Martin Bormann's office in the first room on the right of the corridor, just inside the underground entrance. The large maps were continuously updated by staff to show the routes taken by the enemy bombers. The orders for the German 'suicide' pilots – those willing to sacrifice their lives to fight the Allied air invasion – went out from the office by radio. One such episode is emblematic: on April 7, 1945, 180 Messerschmitt 109s took off from Hanover to intercept a fleet of American bombers. Of the 180, 133 were downed and 77 pilots, who did not manage to eject and parachute from their planes, were killed. The Americans lost 23 bombers.

As soon as Bormann received these appalling statistics they were relayed to the Führer's so-called apartment, which was halfway down the corridor on the left. It consisted of a meeting room with a wooden table and benches, a sitting room with a sofa, a desk and a portrait of Frederick the Great on the wall, and a bedroom where Hitler slept on a cot. Eva Braun's room was further down the hall. Connected by an underground passage to the gloomy hovel where the dying heart of the Third Reich continued to beat was the Voss Bunker, which could hold 2000 people and had been converted into a hospital. This was where pregnant women were brought to give birth. For each child born, Hitler had a bouquet of flowers sent to the mother and a savings book containing 100 marks for the baby.

There was both compassion and brutality. The Führer sent out an order for the immediate execution of any Allied pilots shot down and captured, whether injured or not, but General Koller made it clear that neither the *Luftwaffe* nor the *Sicherheitsdienst* (Security Service) would obey such an order, and Hitler was obliged to accept the situation.

Meanwhile both the Western and Baltic Fronts collapsed. On March 22, the Americans passed over the Rhine on pontoon bridges after the bridge at Remagen had collapsed. On March 24, thousands of German soldiers threw down their arms and deserted when confronted by the British army led by Montgomery. At the end of March, the Wehrmacht abandoned its positions on the Baltic to the Russians, and Kolberg, Danzig and Königsberg fell, one after the other.

These defeats produced fateful consequences in the relations between Hitler and his closest collaborators. It was necessary to find a scapegoat on whom Hitler could vent all his anger and frustration. The Führer's principal confidant was Robert Ley, the chief of the *Arbeitsfront*, who revealed after the war how Hitler lost all confidence in Heinrich Himmler, whom he called "disobedient, dishonest and incompetent." On the other hand, the loyalty of others resulted in the supreme sacrifice, as was the case with Walther Model, commandant of the B Army Corps, who committed suicide to avoid being taken prisoner by the Allies in the Ruhr.

Even Albert Speer, one of Hitler's most faithful followers, decided to disobey his leader's orders to destroy everything in the enemy's path to slow their advance: buildings, wells, aqueducts, bridges and so on. Speer tried to dissuade the Führer, first with a series of memoranda and then, on March 18, by going in person to the bunker. Hitler loved Speer too much to have him shot, but on March 22 he revoked his appointment as Minister of Armaments.

Another famous German officer disappointed Hitler. On April 5, 1945, Heinz Guderian, the successful tank strategist in Poland, France and Russia in 1939-40, had a heated argument with his commander in chief about the defeat suffered by General Busse at Küstrin against the Red Army. Guderian even raised his voice. Hitler made everyone leave the room, then whispered to the commander of the *Panzerdivisionen*, "You need a vacation. Come back in six weeks."

During the interminable evenings Hitler spent in the bunker, Goebbels read him passages from Thomas Carlyle's biography of Frederick the Great, and Jodl continued to believe Hitler was an unrivaled strategist, as he later stated at the Nuremberg trials. His hair had turned gray and his sight had deteriorated to the point that he was obliged to wear glasses even to be able to read documents typed on the special typewriters, with characters three times the usual size, used by his three secretaries. Furthermore, both his hands trembled continuously.

Every now and then he received some good news. On the Eastern Front, the German antitank divisions slowed down the Russian advance to quite a degree. In February 1945, 4600 Soviet tanks were destroyed – at a time when the entire Soviet monthly production did not exceed 2300. In the first three weeks of March, the number of enemy vehicles destroyed rose to 5400. Nonetheless, this did not stop the Russians from reaching the gates of Vienna on April 5.

The question of the *Konzentrationslager* or prison camps and the *Vernichtungslager* – the extermination camps for Jews, Communists and 'inferior' races – had become dramatic. What could be done? Goering suggested they be handed over to the enemy as they were, but the Führer ordered that they be evacuated and that all inmates not strong enough to face the journey were to be killed (this is the version told in Hitler's most benevolent biography, *Hitler's War* by David Irving). A number of important prisoners – Austrian Chancellor Schuschnigg, Dr. Schacht, General Halder, Molotov's nephew, and Captain Payne Best of the British Special Operations Executive – were transported to Bavaria and treated well. Not so Admiral Canaris and

General Oster, conspirators in the July 20 plot, who were hanged in Flossenburg on April 9, 1945.

Hitler had a plan to build a mountain retreat in the Bavarian Alps. On April 9 he ordered the Gauleiter of the Tyrol, Franz Hofer, to set up a series of military installations immediately in the Alto Adige region, though this was formally Italian territory. The commander was to be Kesselring, with Dönitz to command the northern front. On April 12 he called Kesselring. The next day, they heard the unexpected and astonishing news of Roosevelt's death. Dr. Goebbels compared it to the death in 1762 of Czarina Elizabeth, the daughter of Peter the Great, who had made Prussia under Frederick II suffer its darkest hours in the Seven Years' War. "It is the great turnaround!" shouted the Minister of Propaganda, "It is the will of God!" Hitler dictated a proclamation "against the Bolshevik Jews" to be issued immediately to the soldiers on the Eastern Front. It included the phrase, "…. destiny has removed the greatest criminal of all time from the face of the earth."

Two days later, on April 15, Eva Braun, whom Hitler had decided to place safely in Bavaria, returned to Berlin using improvised means, in time to share the anguish that pervaded the bunker at the news of the offensive launched by General Zukov along the Oder-Neisse line. At dawn on April 16, half a million Soviet grenades rained down on the 9th Army of General Busse. In the first few hours of this massive clash, sixty suicide pilots of the Luftwaffe destroyed the bridges over the Oder as they were crossed by the Russians, while the German automatic batteries put 211 Soviet tanks out of commission. But the Red Army was an inexorable tide. Soon General Zukov's troops, which had attacked from the east, were joined by those commanded by Konjev and Rokossowski, from the north and south respectively, in an advance aimed directly at Berlin. The German defenders could only fight and die. The mere thought of surrender was considered betrayal. The following instructions were included in the Führer's order to resist: "Any officer who does not obey this order unquestioningly will be shot immediately." The example came directly from the bunker, where Hitler ordered the arrest and execution of his personal surgeon, Dr. Brandt, guilty of having sent his family to safety in the American zone (Brandt managed to escape capture but was later hanged by the Allies in 1947 for his experiments on camp detainees). One of the names on the list of traitors in those days was that of Reichsmarshall Hermann Goering who, on April 23, sent a telegram from the Obersalzberg, where he had taken refuge three days earlier, daring to ask Hitler permission to "assume leadership of the Reich immediately and completely, with full freedom of action in Germany and abroad, as your deputy." He added, "If I do not receive a reply before 10 p.m. today, I will assume that you have lost your freedom of action and, considering the conditions set out in your decree of June 29, 1941 to be fulfilled, I will act in the best interests of our country and people." Hitler's reaction was to strip Goering immediately of all his responsibilities and order the SS at the *Obersalzberg* to place him under house arrest. His telegram of reply followed: "Your actions are punishable by death, but in consideration of the notable services you have rendered in the past, I will not initiate procedures of that kind."

So, beset by betrayal, frustration and anger, the life of the Führer continued. On April 20, he celebrated his fifty-sixth birthday. He suffered from insomnia and Parkinson's disease. He tried to find some relief spending half an hour at a time with his Alsatians in the kennel behind the toilets, almost always keeping a puppy on his lap. He let off steam in long monologues to four young women: Eva Braun and his three secretaries Traudl Junge, Johanna Wolf and Christa Schröder. Every so often, he climbed

On his 56th birthday, the Führer decorated members of the Hitler Youth for having valorously defended Berlin. This was on April 20, 1945. Ten days later he committed suicide in the bunker.

the spiral staircase to go into the gardens of the Chancellery to bestow awards for valor on the youths of the *Volkssturm* (National Militia) and *Hitlerjugend* (Hitler Youth) defending Berlin.

On April 22, presiding over the War Council, he announced that rather than leave Berlin for the Berchtesgaden refuge in Bavaria, where almost all the high-ranking officers – including Goering – had already gone or were on their way, he would commit suicide. This was the first mention of the subject. The next day he replaced the small pistol he kept in his pocket with a Walther 7.65 that, until then, he had kept locked in his desk drawer. Then he burned all the most important documents in his private archives, choosing them individually and throwing them in the flames. In the days that followed, Bormann, Goebbels, Keitel, Jodl (and, by telephone, Dönitz and Himmler) tried to make him change his mind about suicide. So did Eva Braun, whom Hitler in turn constantly begged to leave Berlin for the Berchtesgaden. According to eyewitnesses, upon hearing her resolute reply, "You know I will never leave you," the greatly moved Hitler burst into tears, kissed her and hugged her.

Not all the top Nazi officers attempted to save themselves. Ribbentrop, for example, asked an armored unit to accept him as a simple recruit so that he could die alongside other troops, but General Weidling prevented this after consulting the Führer. On April 25 the American and Russian troops met at Torgau on the Elbe, a symbolic event that sounded the death knell for the Third Reich. The only hope left for Hitler was the 12th Army under General Wenck and the Germany Army under Field Marshal Schörner, formerly commander of the 4th Panzer Army Corps, which was advancing towards the capital for the last stand.

On April 26 the intrepid aviator Hanna Reitsch flew a training aircraft to Berlin, with the injured General von Greim as passenger, and made an improvised landing on the wide street behind the Chancellery. She hoped to gain glory by carrying the Führer away to safety, but as soon as she was admitted into his presence she understood that she would only offend him by making such a proposal. Hitler took her hands in his, asked her to stay with her airplane ready for any need and promoted Greim to Commander of the *Luftwaffe* in Goering's place.

The dark hours in the bunker were cheered by the smiles and angelic voices of the Goebbels' six children, who sang a song each evening for 'Uncle Adolf' that contained the verse "…we are waiting for the arrival of the soldiers / who will chase the Bolshevik Russians away." The children were called Helga, Hilde, Helmut, Halde, Hedda and Haide: five girls and a boy, whose names all began with an "H", in honor of Hitler.

The worst day in the bunker was undoubtedly April 28, when the Allied radio announced that Himmler, the chief of the Waffen-SS, had made contact with the British and Americans with the aim of unconditional surrender. Himmler had not been seen for days, and all contact between him and Hitler had taken place through Hermann Fegelein, Eva Braun's brother-in-law. That day, Fegelein had managed to speak with Eva by phone and tried to persuade her to save her life. While Eva was in tears, Gestapo agents forced their way into Fegelein's apartment in Kurfürstendamm St., where they found proof of Himmler's treachery and secret funds. Fegelein was handcuffed and taken to the bunker, but Hitler refused to see him, instead ordering that he be taken to the garden and shot immediately. Shortly after, Hitler called Hanna Reitsch and ordered her to take General von Greim to the Reichlin airbase for a last offensive by the *Luftwaffe*, also instructing her to arrest Himmler and have him shot. He then had his favorite dog, Blondi, brought to his room, where he forced her to swallow a cyanide capsule. The dog died almost instantly. Since the cyanide had been given to him by the SS doctor Stumpfegger, and Hitler considered all the SS traitors, he doubted the poison was lethal and had wanted to test its effectiveness.

As Blondi lay dead at the Führer's feet, Bormann strode into the office announcing that Soviet tanks had surrounded Potsdamer Platz and the Russian infantry would break into the Chancellery at any moment. It was at this point that Hitler called in Traudl Junge from Bavaria who, at 25, was the youngest of his secretaries. She and her colleagues referred to the Führer as *'der Chef'*. She later recounted the entire story in her book *Until the Final Hour*, published in February 2002.

"My child", Hitler said to her with a smile, "have you been able to rest a little? I would like to dictate something. No, not for the typewriter. Take a notepad to write down in shorthand." And he dictated to history his political will. He appointed Admiral Dönitz his successor and Field Marshal Schörner Army Commander in Chief. He ordered Dönitz to "continue the war against the poisoner of all nations, international Jewry." Then he announced his decision to marry Eva Braun and, immediately after, to commit suicide with her. Having completed his dictation ("with detachment, almost mechanically," Junge noted), he ordered that three copies of the document be typewritten: one for Dönitz, one for Schörner and the last for his comrades at the Obersalzberg.

The wedding took place at 2 a.m. on April 29. It was very brief. The master of ceremonies was a municipal employee tracked down by Goebbels who, for the occasion, had been asked to wear a *Volksturm* armband. Shortly after, Hitler and Goebbels recalled the years of their struggle for power. Then they went to their rooms for a few hours of fitful sleep until, at noon on April 29, everyone entered Bormann's office where they heard an Italian radio station announcing the public display of the bodies of Mussolini and Claretta Petacci in Piazzale Loreto in Milan. The Russian advance was fought yard by yard by the last defenders of Nazism, the fanatical legions of the SS of different nationalities: German, French, Walloon, Spanish, Tibetan and Muslim. Their resistance helped postpone the final act of the tragedy. Hitler wrote a few letters. In the one to Keitel, he wrote, "Too many persons have abused my trust. Support Dönitz. Disloyalty and betrayal have undermined our capacity to resist. Remember that the aim of Germany must always be to conquer eastern territories."

On the evening of April 29, Hitler decided to say farewell to the women in the bunker and the Voss Bunker: his secretaries, nurses, and the wives of the officers. This thanksgiving was something that Eva Braun had requested. Hitler had words of gratitude for all of them and the women could not hold back their tears.

On the morning of April 30, the Russians broke through into Wilhelmstrasse and Saarlandstrasse in Berlin. The radio receivers allowed Bormann to monitor the end almost yard by yard. Hitler announced he would kill himself at 3 p.m. He shaved calmly and then donned a green shirt, black shoes and a new uniform. He called Bormann and the ordinance officer Otto Günsche and asked them to be ready to give him the *coup de grace*, if necessary, and to cremate his body and Eva Braun's so that they would be reduced to ashes before the arrival of the Russians.

He then had a frugal lunch and invited all the female staff to sit around the table with him. At 3 p.m. he retired with Eva Braun in the sitting room with the green and white walls. The explosions of the Soviet grenades shook the walls. Hitler and Eva sat beside one another on the sofa opposite the portrait of Frederick the Great. The Führer held a photograph of his mother. Each took a phial of cyanide from a small bag. Eva was the first to break it and swallow the contents; she died almost instantly. Hitler held his phial in his left hand and, dropping the photograph on the sofa, took his Walther 7.65 in his right hand. With one last look at Eva's lifeless body beside him, he broke the phial in his teeth and, at the same time, shot himself in the temple.

A few minutes later the two bodies were burned in the hallway as the Hamburg radio station, informed by Bormann, announced to the world, "Our leader has died at his command post in the Reich Chancellery, fighting against Bolshevism and for Germany to the last." Bormann cleared his office and left the bunker to disappear forever. The next day, May 1, Goebbels used cyanide to kill his six children and his wife, and then he ordered a soldier of the SS to shoot him, sprinkle the bodies with gasoline and burn them.

When the Russians entered the bunker on May 2, they found the burnt bodies and a few soldiers who surrendered. Admiral Dönitz left Hamburg and moved the seat of government to Flensburg in the far north of Germany. He was followed by Himmler, who was being sought both by the Allies and those loyal to the Führer. Dressed as a simple soldier but recognized by an American, he took his life by swallowing a capsule of cyanide.

On May 7, 1945, Admiral Dönitz signed the unconditional surrender of Nazi Germany before representatives of the United States and Great Britain in Reims, France. His signature before the representatives of the USSR took place in Berlin on May 9.

A steel bust of Hitler found among the rubble of the Berlin Chancellery. Eva Braun ▶ committed suicide on April 30 by taking cyanide. Immediately after this, Hitler took his life by taking cyanide and at the same time shooting himself in the temple.

CHAPTER 13

NUREMBERG:
THE DAY OF RECKONING

M ore than half a century has not been enough for historians to provide an unequivocal answer to the question of whether the Nuremberg trials were just. In all likelihood, not even a thousand years will suffice. Never has the ancient maxim that "might makes right" been as true as in this crucial historical episode. For the first time in the thousands of years of human history, the leaders of a defeated nation were called by the victors to answer to their behavior and crimes. The reading of the sentences began on the morning of September 30, 1946, in the main courtroom of the Justizpalast in Nuremberg. Twelve were condemned to death, three to life imprisonment, two to twenty-year prison sentences, one to 15 years, one to 10 years and three were absolved. Of the twenty-two accused, only one was not present: Martin Bormann, a leader of the Nazi Party, is thought to have escaped to South America and was never seen again. But the most important characters had escaped trial by taking their own lives: Adolf Hitler had shot himself in the temple in the Chancellery bunker, Joseph Goebbels had an SS soldier kill him after he had poisoned his wife

◄ *Some leaders of the Third Reich during the war crimes trial conducted by the International Military Tribunal of Nuremberg. In the front row of the rear section, from left to right: Hermann Goering, Rudolf Hess, Joachim von Ribbentrop and Wilhelm Keitel. In the second row are Karl Dönitz, Erich Raeder, Baldur von Schirach and Fritz Sauckel. Behind them are the military police.*

Magda and their six children, and Heinrich Himmler, the head of the SS, took cyanide soon after being captured.

The trial of the surviving leaders of the Third Reich began on November 20, 1945. Nuremberg was chosen, as it was the city of the party conventions that had glorified Nazism. The Court consisted of four judges and four assistant judges (one for each of the four Allied powers: the US, the USSR, Great Britain and France) and it was presided over by the English judge Sir Geoffrey Lawrence. The accused had four representatives and sixty lawyers. There were 408 court sessions, 116 witnesses for the prosecution, 101 witnesses for the defense, 143 written depositions, and more than 3000 written documents collected by a commission chaired by the American William Coogan.

The decision to try the Axis leaders was made during the three-way Moscow Conference on October 30, 1943. Of the three leaders (Stalin, Churchill and Roosevelt), only the British prime minister had shown any doubts, but he finally yielded. A list was drawn up of the six political leaders who would have to be tried in the event of an Allied victory: Hitler, as the head of the Nazi Party; Mussolini, as head of the Fascist Party; Himmler, the head of the SS; Goebbels, the German Minister of Propaganda; Goering, Hitler's number two; and Ribbentrop, the German Foreign Minister. In his autobiography, Winston Churchill wrote that with the murder of Mussolini "at least the world was spared an Italian Nuremberg." The crimes to be prosecuted were decided in a series of meetings among the British, American and Russian plenipotentiaries, to whom, after the end of the war, General De Gaulle argued that the French should be added.

Recognizing that a trial of this kind had never been held, that it would clash with the principle of the non-retroactivity of the law, and that, in international law, there existed no standard that could hold ministers and generals responsible for the conduct of a war, the Allied lawyers formulated the accusations around moral principles of a universal nature. Consequently, the indictments contained four counts: 1) crimes against peace (violations of treaties, annexations of States, aggression against neutral countries like Belgium, the Netherlands, etc.; 2) war crimes (the killing of prisoners); 3) crimes against humanity (the genocide of the Jews); 4) "a common plan or conspiracy to commit" the criminal acts listed in the first three counts.

On October 2, 1944, in executing the Moscow agreement, American colonel Burton C. Andrus (later to become the Nuremberg jailer) had been ordered to set up the International Security Detachment and to transform the Palace Hotel in Mondorf-Les-Bains in Luxemburg into a prison for the Nazi defendants. The first to be imprisoned was the former German Chancellor (later Hitler's ambassador to Vienna and Ankara), Franz von Papen. He was followed by the former Foreign Minister Baron von Neurath, and Rudolf Hess, the former secretary of the Nazi Party and Hitler's 'shadow'. Hess was brought from London, where he had been under arrest since 1941 when he parachuted into Scotland in an illusory bid to conclude a separate peace with Britain. Once Germany was fully occupied, the leaders who had already been captured were transferred to the prison in Zellenstrasse, next to the law courts. Here they were gradually joined by others. Hans Frank, the governor general of occupied Poland, was captured at Berchtesgaden near the Austrian border. Although he was not recognized, he panicked because he was in possession of false documents and, well aware of the crimes he had committed, he slit his wrists. When he was given treatment, he admitted his identity. Not expecting to be arrested, Goering gave himself up to the Allies and was taken to Nuremberg on May 7, the day before the signature of Germany's unconditional surrender. On October 18, 1945 in Berlin, an announcement was made to the world of the imminent start of the trial, and there were twenty-one accused. Only Martin Bormann was missing.

On the morning of November 20, the accused were seated on the benches in two rows. Behind them stood white-helmeted Military Policemen and in front sat the defense lawyers, who represented the best German legal firms that had not been compromised by Nazism.

The chief of the public ministers (among whom Russian General Rudenko and Frenchman Charles Dubost distinguished themselves) was the US Justice Robert Jackson, an uncompromising and handsome man of 40. It took the first two days to read the indictment, which was 25,000 words long. Included in the accusations (suppression of freedom, persecution of the Jews, murder of the mentally ill) was the military aggression (in chronological order) of Germany against the Rhineland, Austria, Sudetenland, Czechoslovakia, Poland (though Jackson was very careful to omit the fact that Poland had been attacked simultaneously by the USSR), and finally the USSR on June 21, 1941. A moving chapter in the address was dedicated to the massacre of British and American airmen shot down and captured as they landed by parachute. Jackson said, "Germany did not consider them prisoners of war but criminals, and the soldiers allowed the people to hang them."

The accused were given a list of 300 law firms from which to choose their defense counsel. The leading German lawyers were preferred. The most renowned was undoubtedly Otto Stahmer, Goering's counsel. Old, short, edgy and aggressive, he contested the legitimacy of the international court from the very beginning, invoking the fundamental principle of Roman law *Nulla poena sine lege* (retroactive laws are not permitted), and contesting the right of the victors to try the vanquished. A court composed of neutral countries like Switzerland, Sweden and Spain may have had the right to try the Nazis, "but here," Stahmer added, "in this hall, the States that during the war were on the other side of the fence have done everything. They have compiled the indictment, they have written the criminal law, they are the prosecution and they are the judges." He was wasting his breath. Each objection was rejected by the court.

A deadly blow to the defense was the evidence provided by the former commander of Auschwitz, Rudolf Höss, who was led into the hall on April 11, 1946 after being captured by the Russians (he was hanged in Warsaw in 1947). Höss confirmed the terrible truth of the 'final solution of the Jewish question'. He provided the court with first and last names, as well as a detailed account of how millions of Jews had been eliminated in the gas chambers. The climax was reached on the dramatic day of November 27, 1945, when the Soviet prosecutor Rudenko showed films from the extermination camps: women stripped and massacred, children killed, hell on earth. Judges and journalists held their breath. Keitel wiped his forehead. Dönitz put his face in his hands. Raeder and Speer were dejected. Only Streicher remained unmoved throughout the film. At the end Goering shouted, "You're liars! This is a setup using clever movie tricks!" But Fritzsche commented, "The shame of Germany cannot be erased." Frank cried, "Damn Hitler!" And Keitel commented, "*SS schweinehunde*" ("SS pigs"). Funk, as usual, cried.

To the surprise of the accused, on February 11, 1946 General Friedrich von Paulus appeared. After being defeated at Stalingrad, he had been taken prisoner by the Russians. "Who, among the accused, actively participated in the invasion of the USSR?" Lawrence asked. Paulus turned and pointed to three men: Keitel, Jodl and Goering. But when Baron von Weizsaecker (formerly the Secretary of State and the father of the future President of Germany) told the court about the secret clause of the Ribbentrop-Molotov Pact, concerning the division of six European countries between the Third Reich and the USSR, the court shirked the issue and moved on to another subject. And when the subject of the 10,000 Polish military officers executed by the Soviets at Katyn came up, the court let it drop; it was simply not interested in Communist atrocities.

On September 30, 1946, after a month of seclusion in the counsel chamber (though they ate at restaurants and slept at the hotel), the judges began their reading of the twenty-two sentences, which took two days. The courtroom was connected via radio to loudspeakers in the squares of the most important German cities.

The only one to escape the hangman was Hermann Goering, who had obtained a phial of cyanide (no one ever discovered how). He swallowed the poison shortly before midnight on October 15, as soon as he was told by Commander Andrus that it was time for his execution. Shortly after, the other ten sentenced to die had their wrists tied behind their backs so that they could not follow Goering's example. The executions took place between 1 and 3 a.m. on the morning of October 3. The hangman, American sergeant John C. Woods, was a specialist, as he performed the same duty in the American army and had supervised 347 executions during the war.

The noose around the neck of each dead man was left with the body so there would be no relics for collectors or sympathizers. At 5:30 that morning, the bodies (stripped of their clothes, which were returned to the families) were loaded onto two trucks and transported to the former extermination camp of Dachau, where they arrived three hours later. A former inmate, a knife-grinder from Munich named Richard Wagner, had been assigned to start up one of the furnaces. The corpses were pushed in, one after another. By midday, all that remained was a heap of ashes, which was swept into two trash bins. In the afternoon, soldiers on the bank of the Isar River, which flows through Munich, shoveled the ashes into the water and they floated away with the current.

Hermann Goering speaking with his lawyer, Otto Stahmer, in the Nuremberg prison. ▶
After receiving the death sentence, in order to avoid the humiliation of hanging the Nazi leader committed suicide with a capsule of cyanide he had somehow managed to procure.

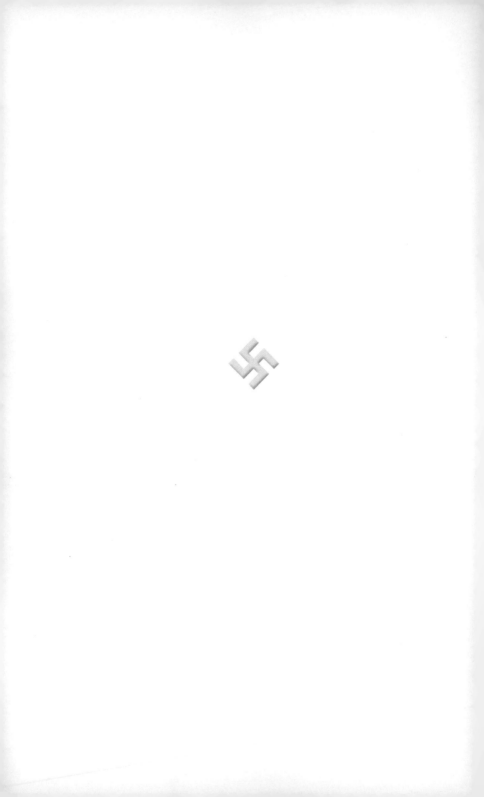

THE FÜHRER'S RELATIONSHIP WITH WOMEN

Adolf Hitler's companion for 12 years who then became his wife a few hours before her death, Eva Braun has to this day been depicted ruthlessly by historians and journalists, who have treated her as an icon devoid of soul, heart and brain. This was certainly not the case. Nevertheless, she shared the bitter fate that was in store for all the women who played an important role in the Führer's life: suicide. Before her, Hitler's beautiful, young niece Geli Raubal had taken her own life. And at almost the same time as Eva's suicide, in the Berlin bunker was the scene of another one, that of Magda Quandt, Goebbel's wife, who had not hesitated to marry the Propaganda Minister to ensure that she would spend her life near Hitler, the man she loved unrequitedly.

Let us begin with Geli Raubal. Geli (short for Angelika) was the youngest daughter of Adolf's half-sister Angela Raubal. Numerous books have been written about this charming, smiling but unfortunate girl with long dark hair (the most recent work, by Ronald Hayman and published in New York in 1997, is *Hitler and Geli*), but no one has ever managed to find con-

◀ *Eva Braun (1910-1945) at the age of 25. Hitler always carried this photograph, with his lover's signature, in a wallet later found by American soldiers.*

vincing proof that, aside from mutual and profound affection, there was any sexual intimacy between the two.

In the summer of 1927, Hitler persuaded his half-sister Angela, who was six years his senior and a widow, to leave Vienna and move to the villa he had rented at Obersalzberg to work as the housekeeper. The resort, famed for winter sports and tourism, was just two hours from Munich by car and very close to the Austrian border. Angela arrived with her daughters, Friedl and Geli. Just 19, Geli had met her uncle in Landsberg in 1924, when she had accompanied her mother to visit him while he was in prison after the Beer Hall Putsch. Geli then enrolled at the university Faculty of Medicine and went to live in a one-room apartment she rented in Munich, where she met and fell in love with Emil Maurice.

Maurice, born in 1897, was the Führer's chauffeur. He was a powerhouse during the scuffles with the Communists, and Hitler nicknamed him 'our greyhound'. Following the unsuccessful Putsch, Maurice was also sentenced and spent nine months at the Landsberg fortress, copying the final version of *Mein Kampf.*

Maurice was formidable behind the wheel and, in his company, Hitler would sometimes go to the Academy of Fine Arts in Munich "to admire the nude models," as his secretary Christa Schröder would later testify. Thus, he was something more than just a chauffeur: he was also a friend and companion. He had always been lucky with women, and had a widely touted two-year relationship with Ada Klein, a journalist with the *Völkischer Beobachter.* In the 1950s Maurice recalled many of

◀ *Angelika Raubal (known as Geli) was the daughter of Hitler's half-sister Angela. She moved to the Wolf's Lair with her mother when Hitler had asked the latter to be his housekeeper. In 1931 the young woman shot herself in the heart with her uncle's pistol.*

his other relationships, selling his memoirs to *Stern* and other tabloids.

When Hitler realized that his niece had a crush on Maurice, he immediately stepped in. He knew his driver too well and was sure that he did not have serious intentions and would hurt the girl. As a result, he demanded that Maurice end the relationship. The rapport between the two deteriorated and during the 1928 Christmas holidays Hitler fired Maurice, who went on to open a watch store in Munich. Hitler had become attached to Geli, and to distract her he took her to Hamburg and Helgoland with Joseph Goebbels and his wife. From then on, Geli became her uncle's steady companion. She followed him to shops, movies, the opera, the theatre, assemblies, party meetings, and appointments with journalists who wanted to interview him. In the fall of 1929, she moved to Adolf's Prinzregentenplatz apartment. Naturally, such a lovely girl did not pass unobserved. Everyone thought the two had fallen in love, although Heinrich Hoffmann, Hitler's photographer who had hired Geli for a certain period of time, always swore that there was deep affection but not sexual love. According to Hoffman, "Hitler wanted to prevent Geli from falling into the hands of a trickster."

The tragedy came to a head after two years of living together. Something had changed in their relationship and they no longer understood each other. Geli, who in the meantime had abandoned her medical studies in Munich, told her uncle she wanted to return to Vienna to resume voice lessons and start a career in operetta. Her uncle forbade her. Out of jealousy or because he wanted her to go back to the university? Heated arguments followed, culminating in a dramatic scene in the presence of numerous witnesses on September 17, 1931. Hitler had gone down the stairs of the house, as a car was waiting to take him and Heinrich Hoffmann to the airport to go to Hamburg for a political rally. She threw open the window and shouted, "So you won't let me go to Vienna?" "No!" responded the Führer. Geli killed herself that night, shooting a bullet through her heart with her uncle's gun.

Alerted by telephone, Hitler dashed back to Munich, hoping to find her alive. When he saw she was dead, he in turn threatened to commit suicide and his closest friends had to take turns watching over him, day and night, to prevent him from doing so. Angela Raubal had her daughter's body brought back to Vienna, where the funeral was held. Hitler found lodgings in the Austrian capital and would weep at Geli's tomb for nights on end. He then decided to punish himself by no longer eating meat (he was already a teetotaler and had never touched tobacco). From that day on, he would always keep a portrait of Geli in his bedroom, and the girl's room at Obersalzberg became a sort of shrine.

Attempted suicide marked the life of a tall, beautiful, blond and romantic English girl, Unity Mitford, who decided to live in Berlin to be near the man she loved and admired, Adolf Hitler. This desperate act left her paralyzed and in atrocious pain for eight years until her death. Unity was the third child of the Count of Redesdale, a member of the House of Lords and a pro-Nazi just like the former king, Edward VIII. And the count transmitted his political leanings to his children. His eldest daughter married Sir Oswald Mosley, founder and head of the British Union of Fascists, and his son had enlisted as a volunteer with Franco's troops during the Spanish Civil War. And Unity, his youngest child, moved to Berlin, where she soon became part of the Führer's inner circle – partly thanks to her beauty. She was present at all the receptions given at the Chancellery and was always a guest of honor in Hitler's box at the Berlin

Opera. Gossip spread quickly: was this the Führer's newfound love? This is hard to say, partly because – officially – Unity had created a club of intellectuals, diplomats and writers whose goal was to prevent a breakdown of relations between Great Britain and Germany. However, in a letter to her father, in whom she regularly confided as she would have done with her closest friend, she wrote, "These months are like a dream."

On September 3, 1939, all her hopes and dreams were suddenly shattered. When she heard the radio announcement that Great Britain had declared war on Germany, Unity, who was visiting Munich, left her hotel, went to the English Garden and shot herself in the temple. Though she survived, the bullet damaged her nerve centers, leaving her paralyzed and unable to speak. As soon as he heard the news, Hitler personally called the best surgeons in the country and sent them to Munich. Every morning, he phoned for an update on the girl's condition. Unity had not lost consciousness and, indeed, was lucid and desperate. She asked one of the nurses who assisted her day and night to bring her the gold medal with the swastika that was a gift from Hitler, and place it on her chest. During a moment of distraction among the nursing staff, Unity swallowed the medal, but this second attempt at suicide also failed. With the help of the International Red Cross, the Count of Redesdale finally managed to have his unfortunate daughter sent to a Swiss hospital. From here, he took her to an English clinic, where she died in 1948.

Unity Midford, the daughter of an English aristocrat who was a Nazi sympathizer, ▶
moved to Berlin when barely over 20 in order to live near the Führer, whom she
admired and loved. When war broke out she tried to commit suicide, but lived for
another 9 years, in great suffering due to her head wound.

Pages and pages have been written about Hitler's ideology, political life and military moves, as well as his love life. There have also been allegations that the Führer was homosexual, a 'legend' that goes back to the operation directed against Röhm (the Night of the Long Knives, described in Chapter 4) and the ensuing decree to eliminate all homosexuals from the NSDAP. In the fall of 1942, journalist Hans Walther Aust, a highly authoritative member of the Reich Press Chamber, was charged with telling the Führer's adjutant, Julius Schaub, that Hitler was hosting a girl (Eva Braun) at Obersalzberg for the sole purpose of concealing his homosexuality. The accusation was leveled against him by Schaub himself. Aust was sentenced to two years in prison, despite the fact that, as the judges noted in the sentence, "the Führer is in too high a position to be harmed by such gossip." Nevertheless, from 1943 on, anyone who circulated rumors of this kind risked the death penalty.

In 2000, Lothar Machtan, a professor of contemporary history at the University of Bremen, was the first to conduct a thorough scientific study of Hitler's presumed homosexuality, as opposed to the psycho-historical study published the previous year by Manfred Koch-Hillebrecht in his *Homo Hitler* (1999, Munich). Machtan examined thousands of pages of records from trials for defamation, rereading memoirs and reports of the interrogations conducted by the Allied commissions and interviewing the survivors. It must be said, by the way, that the subject of homosexuality was taboo until almost the end of the twentieth century.

In his book *The Hidden Hitler*, Machtan maintains that the Führer cold-bloodedly and systematically eliminated all possible sources of revelation. He also accuses Winifred Wagner of destroying extremely valuable documents and Albert Speer of having diverted public attention from the fact that Hitler was sexually attracted to him (supposedly the reason that Hitler did not have Speer killed when, towards the end, he openly disobeyed the Führer's 'scorched earth' decree).

To back his arguments, Machtan relies on the interviews and memoirs of the members of Hitler's entourage who survived the final purge: August Kubizek, Kurt Lüdecke, Putzi Hanfstängl, Eugen Dollmann and Hitler's secretary Christa Schröder. None of them ever make explicit declarations, however; they simply allude, suggest and insinuate. On this basis, Machtan asserts – though this smacks of psychohistory – that as of 1927, Hitler was involved with women solely to conceal his true homosexuality. The proof? Here is one example, if such it can be called: according to Machtan, the fact that Hitler had numerous homes proves that he led a double life. But he might also have had a number of homes to escape attempts on his life. A further allegation by Machtan was that during the Röhm operation, Hitler also ordered that other witnesses of his homosexuality be eliminated, a drastic measure intended to intimidate potential informers or blackmailers. Again, the fierce persecution of homosexuals was, according to this author, a way of clouding public opinion, but it was also linked to Hitler's schizophrenia, as he was unable to rid himself of the unnerving and draining need to hide his homosexuality. Despite appearances, however, these are not convincing arguments.

Now we come to Eva Braun. Born in Munich at the end of 1910, the third child of Fritz Braun, a well-regarded artisan from Simbach am Inn, Eva was a salesclerk and model in the photography studio of Heinrich Hoffman, one of three Nazi militants – together with Ernst Röhm and Rudolf Hess – who were on intimate terms with Hitler. On September 17, 1931 Hitler was traveling with Hoffmann when he received the news that his niece Geli Raubal had committed suicide. For weeks,

this was naturally the main topic of conversation at Hoffmann's studio. Therefore Eva heard Hoffmann's descriptions of Hitler's despair and the fear that the Nazi leader might wish to follow his beloved to the hereafter.

The tension became almost pathological. One evening, Hoffmann said to Eva, "I'm going to see him. Do you want to come?" Angela, Adolf's half-sister and Geli's mother, was unable to continue living in the apartment where Geli had taken her life and had moved to Hitler's chalet, the Berghof, at the Obersalzberg. As Hitler needed a woman to take care of him and keep his house in order, he asked if Eva wanted to take on this role. The tall, slim, good-looking blonde did not hesitate, though she was 22 years younger than Hitler.

At first it was a stormy relationship. There is no doubt that something more than friendship existed between them, perhaps even more than mutual need, but the evident love that Eva felt for the future Führer was not requited, at least not with the intensity the girl would have liked. And this was the motive for her first, theatrical suicide attempt in the summer of 1932, a 'show' aimed at binding to her the man who perhaps did not want a stable relationship. There was to be a second attempt in 1935 (she wounded herself in the shoulder with a pistol shot), due probably to the tense relations between Eva and Angela Raubal, who found it difficult to accept Eva's place in her half-brother's affections. Then Angela left the Berghof for Vienna and Eva settled permanently in the Eagle's Nest. Here

◄ Top *Adolf Hitler and Eva Braun at the 'Eagle's Nest', in the Bavarian Alps, in 1939, with their beloved dogs. The Führer loved German shepherds.*

Bottom *Hitler and Eva in 1938, again at the 'Eagle's Nest'. She and the German dictator were inseparable for years. The young Eva was beautiful and athletic, and loved to hike in the mountains and ski in the winter.*

she lived an apparently carefree life, which consisted of sports (skiing and swimming), looking after the pets, going to the cinema, buying clothes, and organizing lunches and dinners at the mountain inn. She was neither cultured nor interested in politics, and this was the very thing Hitler found attractive. He would spend relaxing and peaceful hours in her company at the Berghof.

After the war there was a race to see who could publish or sell the most stories about her and her tragic love for Hitler, and it was all to the good if, through Eva, the Nazi leader could be demonized even beyond his incontrovertibly perverse nature. Journalists and government services alike were used to achieve this objective. In the summer of 1945 the American press, followed by the rest of the world, announced that Eva Braun's diary had been found by the US Military Police in the rooms of the RHSA (the Reich Security Central Office). This was not the original, but a typed carbon copy that had no handwritten corrections. It contained harrowing stories. One of these told of a crush that Eva had on a certain Kurt, a good-looking, young Viennese painter. When Hitler discovered the affair, he forced Eva to go with him by car to the street in Munich where the young man lived. They got out and went up to the third floor together, where Hitler killed the man with a revolver. Then he had Kurt's 67-year-old father shut up in Dachau, while other relatives were sent to Theresienstadt. Finally, to eliminate every trace of the murder, he had all their names removed from official records, and all the SS officers who had been involved in the operation were assigned to a disciplinary company from which no one ever returned.

Since there is a limit even to the credulity of the simple-minded, the diary operation ended up being counterproductive. Then, mysteriously, some time later the 'original' version (the handwritten copy) of the diary appeared, produced by an artist who lived in Kitzbühl and claimed he had received it from Eva herself, the artist's secret friend, and that he had kept it in a drawer for years before eventually handing it over to American journalist Douglas Hewlett. In her 'diary' Eva naturally described the torments of her love, one of which was that Hitler suffered from phimosis of the penis, which prevented him from having complete sexual relations. She tried to persuade him to have an operation but he refused "because it was too similar to the circumcision of the Jews."

Even on a less substandard level than these attempts to demonize the defeated and dead tyrant (which nonetheless were published around the world as sensational scoops), Hitler's sex life continued to make news for years. Perhaps to regain some credit, Heinrich Hoffman, saved from the purges at Nuremberg, also turned his hand at this. According to a 1954 interview with the *Münchener Illustrierte,* he declared that the relationship between Hitler and the former model had only been platonic and that Eva had never had a fling with a young man, as she would never have betrayed the Führer. Eugen Dollmann, the interpreter between Hitler and the chief Italian Fascists, made the same claim in his book *Roma Nazista* (Nazi Rome; Milan, 1949) when he referred to several conversations he had had with Eva Braun, during which the woman confided in him (though why she would confide in Dollman is not explained) that she and the Führer never had sex "because Hitler is a saint and the idea of physical contact for him would be like sullying his mission." In short, the revelations on the tragic love affair between Adolf and Eva alternated between the ludicrous and the grotesque, at least until the Führer's valet, Heinz Linge, decided to dictate his memoirs (as did the Duce's valet, Pietro Carradori, a few years later).

In his book, *Bis zum Ende* (With Hitler to the End), Linge recounts the bullying to which he was subjected during imprisonment by the Russians who – no less than the Americans – claimed he had made revelations about Hitler's sexual perversions. Linge could only state that the sexual relations between the couple were normal, like those of any loving couple. And he went to great lengths to describe their intimacy, which sometimes included untranslatable nicknames that Hitler gave to Eva, such as 'Schnacksi' and 'Patscherl'.

The young and sporty Eva would have preferred that Hitler dress more informally. "Can't we convince him to wear simpler clothes?" she said one day to Linge. "He always goes around dressed like a policeman." The valet took a hand in the matter and one morning he substituted the Führer's heavy cap with one that was similar but more informal and, above all, not as heavy. Hitler's response was "Linge! Get out my *'Deckel'* (cover) immediately! I'm the one who has to wear it, not Eva." Few knew that the hat – which weighed six pounds – was reinforced with metal to protect Hitler in the event of an assassination attempt.

What lay behind the indissoluble relationship between Hitler and the greatest woman film director in the 20th century was not romantic love, but rather extraordinary empathy. Helene Bertha Amalie 'Leni' Riefenstahl was born in Berlin on August 22, 1902. Her father, Alfred Riefenstahl, was a well-to-do businessman and her mother, Bertha Sherlach, was a former seamstress. Her brother Heinz was born three and half years later; he would die on the Russian front in 1944.

Leni lived in the family apartment on Prinz-Eugen-Strasse until she was 21, when, against her father's wishes, she began to study painting and ballet. She was immediately successful as a ballerina, performing in Berlin, Munich and Prague.

A knee injury interrupted her promising career as a dancer, but the volcanic Leni refused to be discouraged and, following a successful major operation, she enthusiastically tackled her new artistic passion: mountain films.

Mesmerized by the movie poster for Arnold Fanck's film *Berg des Schicksals* (Mountain of Destiny), Riefenstahl went to see the film night after night, until she finally managed to meet the famous director in Berlin. Within a matter of months, she had made such an impression on him that in 1926 she starred in his movie *Der heilige Berg* (The Holy Mountain).

After starring in other 'mountain films' with Luis Trenker, Riefenstahl finally discovered her true vocation: directing. In a field dominated almost exclusively by men, in 1932 Leni emerged as an actress and director in *Das Blaue Licht* (The Blue Light), in which she played the role of Junta, a gypsy girl who climbs Crystal Mountain. However, the years in the Alps, climbing mountains and filming peaks and glaciers, were about to end. Awaiting her was a momentous encounter that would change her life forever.

In 1933, Chancellor Adolf Hitler, as captivated by one of her films as was his Propaganda Minister Joseph Goebbels, called her to Berlin. The Führer wanted her to make a documentary on the National Socialist Convention in Nuremberg. Declaring that she knew nothing about the Nazi ideology and that she was uninterested in politics, Leni accepted nevertheless. Though 'Fräulein Riefenstahl' considered the film a simple and impartial description of what was happening in Germany during that period, her film conveyed such grandeur and artistry that it achieved the very goal Hitler had hoped for: it created the most powerful propaganda medium of the Nazi regime.

The Nuremberg trilogy consists of three separate documentaries. The first, *Sieg des Glaubens* (Victory of Faith), was lost

Appendix 1

during WWII. The second and best-known one, *Triumph des Willens* (Triumph of the Will), won a number of film awards around the world, including a gold medal in Venice in 1935 and the Grand Prix at the international exhibition in Paris in 1937. In it, scenes of mass pageantry, parades and shots of the nighttime assemblies celebrate the power and popularity of the Reich. Lastly, the third documentary, *Tag der Freiheit – Unsere Wehrmacht* (Day Of Freedom: Our Armed Forces), is a glorification of the Führer's military apparatus. The power of the images alone, without any commentary whatsoever, does indeed spill over into art, but it is an art that most certainly served the cause of Nazi Germany.

In 1936, the International Olympic Committee appointed Riefenstahl to film the Berlin Olympics. The result was *Olympia*, which is a celebration of beauty and physical harmony. Divided into two parts, *Fest der Völker* (Festival of the Nations) and *Fest der Schönheit* (Festival of Beauty), *Olympia* won first prize in Venice in 1938 and the ICO Olympic Prize in 1939. The poetry of her images blends with technical perfection, making this work the quintessence of sports filming that is unsurpassed even today. Riefenstahl used a crew of 60 cameramen, creating spectacular aerial shots, sequences effected by running a motorized camera down tracking shot rails to follow the athletes' speed and movements, unprecedented angle shots and slow-motion sequences. Every aspect celebrates and exalts the athletic gestures of the perfect 'Aryan' youth cherished by the Führer.

Leni Riefenstahl (1902-2003), the director of the movie Tieflan *(Loswlands), shot in* ▶ *the early 1940s. She became famous for the three documentaries on the Nuremberg Nazi rallies, and after the war was imprisoned for three years for Nazi propaganda. She was extremely active until her death at the age of 101.*

262

Riefenstahl always vigorously denied that she had even suspected the existence of concentration camps, which had been created to eliminate anything that could mar the Nazi ideal of 'perfection'. The fact remains that Hitler admired Leni enormously and trusted her completely. This is demonstrated in his words, as set down by Martin Bormann in his book *Secret Conversations*: "There have been four women to whom I have entrusted a starring role: Mrs. Troost, Mrs. Wagner, Mrs. Scholtz-Klink and Leni Riefenstahl."

But the great German dream was about to come to an end. The world was at the edge of a cliff, on the verge of war, and with war would come the end of Leni's film career. She was to pay dearly for her friendship with Hitler.

Between 1945 and 1948 the director lived under house arrest for Nazi propaganda and she was also sent to various prison camps. Officially cleared of these charges in 1949, she continued to be accused of being a Nazi sympathizer and had to abandon the movie industry, despite the fact that she had been involved with the regime for only two years.

Even in the case of her last film *Tiefland* (Lowlands), which was shot in the early 1940s but did not come out until 1954, Riefenstahl was accused of recruiting extras from a gypsy lager in Salzburg, an accusation from which she was later exonerated.

Riefenstahl subsequently devoted many years to photography, completing important works of photojournalism on the Nuba tribe of Africa. In 2000, when she was 97, she traversed Sudan in a helicopter in order to help this beloved population, which had been isolated due to the civil war raging there. During her return trip the helicopter crashed due to a technical hitch; Leni miraculously survived, although she was seriously injured. Not even the consequences of this terrible accident could check the volcanic nature of this artist. In 2002, when she was 100 and many years after she had been forced to abandon filmmaking, Riefenstahl directed a film on underwater flora and fauna, which she shot herself thanks to the scuba diving certificate she had been awarded at the age of 72!

Leni Riefensthal died in Germany on September 8, 2003, at the age of 101. But even after her death her memory continued to be tainted somewhat by her relationship with Nazism. Indeed, although such leading Hollywood figures as actress and director Jodie Foster and director and producer Steven Soderbergh wanted to make a movie of her life, these projects were never realized.

LEADING HISTORIANS' VIEWS ON NAZI GERMANY AND THE FÜHRER

RAYMOND CARTIER

Raymond Cartier (1904-75), French journalist and expert in international politics as well as the author of highly regarded works on Adolf Hitler and World War Two. Among the most popular of these is Hitler et ses généraux *(1962).*

"I hated the Nuremberg trial in itself. Certainly not out of sympathy for the 21 defendants: they could have fallen under machinegun fire without stirring the least compassion in me. But to judge them, Justice herself would have had to be called to Nuremberg. Instead, they were being judged without laws, with the pretext of creating, in so doing, a body of laws that was none other than the old *vae victis* [woe to the defeated].... It was quite singular to find among the judges two subjects of a man like Stalin who had ordered the extermination of the Polish officers of Katyn to decapitate Poland. What was needed was a defense attorney willing to stand up and object to those two Soviet judges, two generals who, from their uniforms to their wide epaulets and their very faces, seemed to be made of painted

◀ *A 1928 photograph taken by Hitler's personal photographer Heinrich Hoffmann depicting his typical orator's bearing.*

wood. But the poor German lawyers who were assigned to the defendants were frightened to death. All the president had to hear was the slightest allusion to the German-Soviet pact of 1939 and his gavel would fall to signify that that issue was off-limits. Nuremberg was an instrument of vendetta that was necessary and perhaps understandable in the era and circumstances in which it took place. But it was merely the parody of a court of law.... As to Hitler, all his early campaigns – Poland, Norway, France, the Balkans – demonstrated the fertility of his imagination, his range of resources, his insight into his adversaries, his very realistic knowledge of men and weapons. He subsequently lost the perception of what is possible, he believed in the irresistible power of his will and denied the factors of climate and soil, soldiers' fatigue, the wear and tear of the nation. He froze an army in front of Moscow, he had another one captured at Stalingrad, and he managed to arrange things so that all he had left was a handful of invalids and boys to defend his capital, while his crack divisions still occupied Lombardy and North Cape."

(*Les secrets de la guerre dévoilés à Nuremberg.* Athème Fayard, Paris 1946 [first edition]; *Hitler et ses généraux. Athème Fayard*, Paris 1962 [second edition])

LORD RUSSELL

Edward Frederick Langley Russell, 2nd Baron Russell of Liverpool (1895-1981) was a British soldier, lawyer and historian. He fought in both World Wars and is the author of The Scourge of the Swastika: A Short History of Nazi War Crimes *(1954).*

"The reduction of millions of men to slavery, the murder and torture of prisoners of war, the mass execution of civilians, the shooting of hostages and prisoners as reprisal, and "the final solution of the Jewish question": all this was the outcome of a long-term plan. There is enough proof to erase any doubt, and the Germans themselves have provided it incontrovertibly with their registers, inventories, orders and other documents, all of which were preserved with the greatest care and which fell into the hands of the Allies following the surrender of the German troops in Europe."

(*The Scourge of the Swastika.* Cassel & Co., Ltd. London 1954)

INDRO MONTANELLI

Indro Alessandro Raffaello Montanelli (1909-2001) was the most famous and highly regarded 20th-century Italian journalist. An unsurpassed author of popularized history books, he wrote dozens of works together with such authors as Mario Cervi, Roberto Gervaso, Paolo Granzotto and Marcello Staglieno. The three-volume Terzo Reich. Storia del nazismo *(The Third Reich. History of Nazism) was published in 1965.*

"The history of the Third Reich is the story of a great deception in which, as is always the case with this kind of thing, it is very difficult to distinguish the deceivers from the deceived, many of whom played both roles. The only thing that can be said with any certainty is that, in order to get a grasp of this, one must first of all set aside the grotesque information that has acted as a kind of propaganda that merely perpetuates mutual misunderstandings. Six hundred thousand Germans (without counting the Jews, which is a separate story) died in Nazi extermination camps. The fact that no one talks about this, even in Germany, does not diminish the scope and meaning of this sacrifice."

(*Il Terzo Reich – Storia del nazismo* [The Third Reich. The History of Nazism] Sadea Editore, Florence 1965).

DAVID IRVING

David John Cawdell Irving (1938), British essayist, author of numerous works on World War Two, including The Destruction of Dresden *(1963),* Hitler's War *(1977) and* Churchill's War, Volume I *(1987). Considered a Holocaust denier, he spent 400 days in an Austrian prison for "National Socialist activities."*

"Hitler was a problem, a puzzle, even to his intimate advisers.... The sheer complexity of that character is evident from a comparison of his brutality in some respects with his almost maudlin sentimentality and stubborn adherence to military conventions that others had long abandoned. We find him cold-bloodedly ordering a hundred hostages executed for every German occupation soldier killed; dictating the massacre of Italian officers who had turned their weapons against German troops in 1943; ordering the liquidation of Red Army commissars, Allied commando troops and capture Allied aircrews.... Yet.... he had opposed every suggestion for the use of poison gases, as that would violate the Geneva Protocol.... [W]e learn that Hitler.... not only *never* resorted to the assassination of foreign opponents but flatly forbade his Abwehr to attempt it. In particular, he rejected Admiral Canaris' plans to assassinate the Red Army General Staff."

(*Hitler's War.* Parfoce, London 1977. Revised edition 2001)

WILLIAM SHIRER

William Lawrence Shirer (1904-93). American journalist and historian who stayed in Germany and witnessed the rise of the Third Reich until 1940. He returned to Germany to see the Nuremberg trial. Among his works are Berlin Diary *(1941) and* Rise and Fall of the Third Reich *(1960).*

"Adolf Hitler is probably the last of the great adventurer-conquerors in the tradition of Alexander, Caesar and Napoleon, and the Third Reich the last of the empires which set out on the path taken earlier by France, Rome and Macedonia. The curtain was rung down on that phase of history, at least, by the sudden invention of the hydrogen bomb, of the ballistic missile and of rockets that can be aimed to hit the moon.

".... The remaining intimate collaborators of Hitler lived a bit longer. I went down to Nuremberg to see them. I had often watched them in their hour of glory and power at the annual party rallies in this town. In the dock before the International Military Tribunal they looked different. There had been quite a metamorphosis. Attired in rather shabby clothes, slumped in their seats fidgeting nervously, they no longer resembled the arrogant leaders of old. They seemed to be a drab assortment of mediocrities. It seemed difficult to grasp that such men, when last you had seen them, had wielded such monstrous power, that such as they could conquer a great nation and most of Europe."

(The *Rise and Fall of the Third Reich*. Simon & Schuster, New York 1960).

JOACHIM FEST

Joachim Clemens Fest (1926-2006), journalist and historian, is considered the most important German scholar of Nazism and the Third Reich. Among his major works: Hitler. A Biography *(1974) and* Inside Hitler's Bunker: the Last Days of the Third Reich *(2003), which was the basis of the German film* Downfall.

"No one else produced, in a solitary course lasting only a few years, such incredible accelerations in the pace of history. No one else so changed the state of the world and left behind such a wake of ruins as he did. It took a coalition of almost all the world powers to wipe him from the face of the earth in a war lasting nearly six years, to kill him – to quote an officer of the German Resistance, 'like a mad dog.'

"....However, Hitler also embodied the protest that had long been building up against the haughty selfishness of big capital, against the depraved blend of bourgeois ideology and material interests. He considered Europe as distorted and swallowed up by American capitalism without soil on the one hand and by 'inhuman' Soviet Bolshevism on the other. The essence of his action has rightly been defined as 'the life-and-death struggle.' When all is said and done, Hitler can be understood as an attempt to establish a sort of third force between the two dominant powers of the era, between Left and Right, between East and West.

"The future horrified him. He was delighted – as he said at the evening meal in the Führerhauptquartier – that he had been destined for this experience only at the beginning of the technological era; the generations that followed would no longer know 'how beautiful the world once was.' Despite all his progressive actions, Hitler was a profoundly backward soul, attached above all to the images, standards and inspirations of the nineteenth century, which in his eyes – alongside classical antiquity – was the most significant period in all human history. Even his end, as theatrical a failure as it may appear to be, reflects the two faces of the era he admired: a bit of that ominous splendor that was expressed in the 'twilight of the gods' type of motivations of the planned collapse, but also some of his humbug, expressed by his being stretched out on the sofa in the bunker, next to his faithful mistress, in the pose of the Belle Epoque failed adventurer."

(*Hitler: A Biography.* Harcourt Brace Jovanovic, New York 1974).

ALAN BULLOCK

Alan Charles Louis Bullock (1914-2004), British historian and the author of the first important biography of Adolf Hitler: Hitler: a Study in Tyranny *(1952). In 1993 he published* Hitler and Stalin: Parallel Lives.

"Luck and the disunity of his opponents will account for much of Hitler's success as it will of Napoleon's – but not for all. He began with few advantages, a man without a name and without a support other than that which he acquired for himself, not even a citizen of the country he aspired to rule. To achieve what he did Hitler needed – and possessed – talents out of the ordinary which in sum amounted to political genius, however evil its fruits…. Cynical and calculating in the exploitation of his histrionic gifts, he retained an unshakable belief in his historic role and in himself as a creature of destiny…. The British and French at Munich; the Italians, Germany's partners in the Pact of Steel; the Poles, who stabbed the Czechs in the back over Teschen; the Russians, who signed the Nazi-Soviet Pact to partition Poland, all thought they could buy Hitler off, or use him to their own selfish advantage. They did not succeed, just as the German Right and the German Army also failed."

(*Hitler, a Study in Tyranny*, Odham Books, London 1952)

Essential Bibliography

BULLOCK Alan, *Hitler, a Study in Tyranny*. Odham Books, London 1952 (first ed.).

CARTIER Raymond, *Hitler et ses généraux*. Athème Fayard, Paris 1946.

DOLLMANN Eugen, *Roma nazista*. Longanesi, Milan 1951.

FEST Joachim, *Hitler: A Biography*. New York: Harcourt Brace Jovanovich, 1974. Original title *Hitler. Eine biographie*, Frankfurt am Main – Berlin – Vienna, 1973.

FEST Arnaldo, *La Germany in camicia bruna*. Bompiani, Milan 1937.

GALLO Max, *Night of the Long Knives*. Macmillan, New York 1974. Original title *La nuit des longs couteaux*. Paris, 1970.

GOEBBELS Joseph, *The Goebbels Diaries, 1942-1943*. Greenwood Publishing Group, Westport (CT) (reprint: 1984). Original title *Tagebücher aus den Jahren 1942-43*. Zurich, 1948.

GOEBBELS Daniel Jonah, Hitler's *Willing Executioners: Ordinary Germans and the Holocaust*. Alfred Knopf, New York 1996.

IRVING David, *Hitler's War*. Parforce, London 1977 (new edition 2001).

LÖWENSTEIN Hubertus von, *La Résistance allemande*. Grafes, Bad Godesberg 1966.

MACHTAN Lothar, *The Hidden Hitler*. Basic Books, New York 2001. Original title *Hitlers Geheimnis*. Alexander Fest Verlag, Berlin 2001.

MANN Golo, *The History of Germany since 1789*. Penguin, Harmondsworth 1988. Original title *Deutsche Geschichte des 19. und 20. Jahrhunderts*". Fischer Verlag, Frankfurt a. Main 1958.

MANN Roger & FRANKEL Heinrich, *Doctor Göbbels: His Life and Death*. Heinemann Ltd., London 1960.

MARABINI Jean, *La vie quotidienne à Berlin sous Hitler*. Hachette, Paris 1985.

MASER Werner, *Hitler's Letters and Notes*. Heinemann Ltd., London 1974. Original title *Hitlers Briefe und Notizen*. Econ Verlag, Düsseldorf 1973.

MAYDA Giuseppe, *Norimberga*. Longanesi, Milan 1966.

MONTANELLI Indro (ed.), *Il Terzo Reich – Storia del nazismo* (3 volumes). Sadea Editore, Florence 1965.

POLIAKOV Léon, *Bréviaire de la haine: le III Reich et les Juifs*. Paris, 1952.

REIMANN Victor, *Joseph Goebbels: The Man Who Created Hitler*. Doubleday, Garden City (NY) 1974. Original title *Dr. Joseph Göbbels*. Fritz Molden Verlag, Vienna-Munich 1971.

RITTER Gerhard, *German Resistance: Carl Goerdeler's Struggle against Tyranny*. Praeger, New York 1958. Original title *Carl Gördeler und die deutsche Wiederstandbewegung*. Deutscher Verlag, Stuttgart 1958.

ROTHFELS Hans, *The German Opposition to Hitler*. Regnery, Hinsdale 1948. Original title *Die deutsche Opposition gegen Hitler*. Fischer Bücherei, Frankfurt am Main 1958.

RUSSELL Lord, *The Scourge of the Swastika.* Cassell & Co., London 1954.

SCHLABRENDORFF Fabian von, *Secret War against Hitler,* Pitman, New York 1965. Original title *Offiziere gegen, Hitler.* Zurich, 1947.

SCHOLL Inge, *The White Rose.* Wesleyan University Press, Hanover (NH) 1983. Original title *Die Weisse Rose.* Fischer Bücherei, Frankfurt am Main 1957.

SCHRAMM Percy Ernst, *Hitler, the Man and the Military Leader.* Academy Chicago Publishers, Chicago 1999. Original title *Hitler als militärischer Führer.* Bernard u. Gräfe Verlag, Frankfurt am Main 1961.

SHIRER William, *The Rise and Fall of the Third Reich.* Simon & Schuster, New York 1960.

SMOLEN Kazimierz, *Auschwitz 1940-45.* Oswiecim, 1972.

SPEER Albert, *Spandau: The Secret Diaries.* Harper Collins, New York 1976. Original title *Spandauer Tagebücher.* Verlag Ullstein, Frankfurt am Main 1975.

SPEER Albert, *The Slave State.* Weidenfeld and Nicolson, London 1981. Original title *Der Sklaverstaat.* Deutsche Verlags-Anstalt, Stuttgart 1981.

SPEER Albert, *Inside the Third Reich.* Collier, New York 1970. Original title *Erinnerungen.* Verlag Ullstein, Frankfurt am Main 1969.

WHEELER-BENNET John W., *The Nemesis of Power.* Macmillan & Co., London 1954.

WIESENTHAL Simon, *Murderers among Us: The Simon Weisenthal Memoirs.* McGraw-Hill, New York 1967.

Index

Index

Chancellery bunker, Berlin, 19, 221, 222, 223, 224, 225, 226, 227, 229, 231, 232, 237, 247, 274
Charlemagne, 98
Charles XII of Sweden, 160
Chelmno concentration camp, 188
Chemnitz, 221
Chichester, 215
Christian X of Denmark, 155
Churchill, Winston, 19, 98, 99, 100, 145, 155, 157, 158, 215, 221, 238
Ciano, Galeazzo, 109
Collins, Michael, 166
Cologne, 182
Compiègne, 17, 156
Condor Legion, 131
Coogan, William, 238
Costa, Angelo, 115
Coventry, 157
Cripps, Richard Stafford, 98
Czechoslovakia, 17, 127, 133, 144, 145, 146, 147, 162, 196, 197, 198, 240

D

Dachau concentration camp 15, 83, 180, 242, 258
Dahlem, 202
Daladier, Édouard, 145, 198
Damascus, 175
Danube River, 26
Danzig, 51, 125, 127, 147, 223
DAP (Deutsche Arbeiterpartei or German Workers Party), 46, 48, 49, 50
Daranowsky, Gerda, 146
Darré, Walther Richard, 77
De Felice, Alessandro, 10
De Gaulle, Charles, 157, 163, 238
De Gobineau, Joseph Arthur, 33
Death's Head Hussars, 75
Delmer, Sefton, 39
Delp, Alfred, 211, 216
Denmark, 17, 155
Deutscher Kampfbund, 58
"Deutschland" cruiser, 80
Diels, Rudolf, 72, 73
Dietrich, Sepp, 82, 84
Dimitrov, Georgi, 73
Dirksen, Herbert von, 141
DNVP (Deutschenationale Volkspartei or German National People's Party), 63
Döberitz infantry school, 205
Döllersheim, 24
Dollfuss, Engelbert, 83, 127, 128, 141
Dollmann, Eugen, 255, 259

Donegani, Guido, 115
Donetz Basin, 160
Dönitz, Karl, 225, 228, 230, 231, 232, 237, 241
Dopolavoro, 115
Dornberger, Walther, 164, 165
Dornier airplane factory, 153
Dresden, 157, 221, 272
Drexler, Anton, 14, 46, 47, 50, 52
Dubost, Charles, 240
Duisburg, 222
Dulles, Allen, 214
Dunkirk, 155
Dunstan, Simon, 10

E

Ebert, Friedrich, 46, 62
Eckart, Dietrich, 48, 49, 52, 55
Edward VIII, 154, 251
Egypt, 175
Eichmann, Adolf, 185
Einstein, Albert, 107, 114, 165
Eisner, Kurt, 177
El Alamein, 161
Elbe River, 228
Eldorado,78
Elizabeth of Russia, 225
Ellis, Havelock, 107
Elser, Johann Georg, 153
Enabling Act, 15, 76, 179, 215
English Channel, 155
Ernst, Karl, 73, 78, 79
Esser, Hermann, 55, 57
Estonia, 148
Ethiopia, 125, 130
Europe, 8, 11, 19, 66, 89, 97, 99, 129, 132, 146, 154, 158, 162, 174, 175, 185, 201, 271, 273, 274

F

Falkenhausen, Alexander von, 212
Fallersleben, 116
Fanck, Arnold, 261
Fascist Grand Council, 18
Feder, Gottfried, 48
Frederick II of Prussia (Frederick the Great), 74, 109, 222, 224, 225, 231
Fegelein, Hermann, 229
Feldhernhalle, Munich, 59
Fellgiebel, Fritz Erich, 202, 204, 212
Fest, Joachim Clemens, 12, 50, 273
Figli della lupa, 114
Finland, 148
Flanders, 155
Flensburg, 232
Flossenburg concentration camp, 180, 225

Ford, Henry 116
Fort Banks, 166
Francis Ferdinand, Archduke of Austria, 33
Franz Joseph, Emperor, 23
France, 17, 18, 84, 92, 120, 126, 127, 129, 130, 131, 133, 137, 144, 147, 148, 154, 155, 157, 163, 175, 179, 198, 200, 210, 238, 270, 273
Franco, Francisco, 131, 251
François-Poncet, André, 51, 84
Franconia, 56
Frank, Hans, 187, 190, 191, 239, 241
Frankfurt, 119
Frauenfeld, Alfred Eduard, 127
Freeman-Mitford, David (Count of Redesdale), 251, 252
Freikorps (Free Corps), 46, 55, 56, 177
Freisler, Roland, 210, 211, 213
Freud, Sigmund, 107, 114
Freytag-Loringhoven, Wessel von, 213
Frick, Wilhelm, 57
Fritsch, Werner von, 80, 82, 132, 137, 139, 140
Fritzsche, Hans, 241
Fromm, Friedrich, 201, 206, 208, 209, 213
Funk, Walther, 140, 241

G

Galen, Clemens August von, 216
Galicia, 162
Galilee, 101
Gästebaracke, 202, 203, 204
Gasthof zum Pommer, Braunau-am-Inn, 23
Gauguin, Paul, 109
Generalität, 79, 137
Geneva Protocol, 272
Germany, 10, 11, 15, 16, 17, 18, 33, 37, 39, 45, 49, 54, 55, 57, 61, 63, 64, 65, 66, 67, 72, 75, 76, 82, 89, 92, 97, 107, 109, 114, 115, 116, 120, 125, 126, 127, 128, 129, 130, 131, 132, 137, 139, 144, 145, 148, 149, 153, 154, 155, 156, 158, 161, 162, 163, 171, 176, 177, 178, 179, 180, 182, 184, 187, 188, 191, 195, 197, 198, 199, 200, 201, 208, 209, 212, 215, 226, 231, 232, 239, 240, 241, 252, 261, 262, 264, 265, 271, 272, 275

Index

Index

Index

Photographic Credits

Popperfoto/Getty Images: p. 5
Photo12/IG/Getty Images: p. 9
Keystone/Hulton Archive/Getty
    Images: p. 13
Popperfoto/Getty Images: p. 22
Time Life Pictures/Mansell/Time Life
    Pictures/Getty Images: p. 36
Hulton Archive/Getty Images: p. 38
Popperfoto/Getty Images: p. 4
Imagno/Getty Images): p. 47 top
Hulton Archive/Stringer/Getty Images:
    p. 47 bottom
Imagno/Thomas Sessler Verlag/Getty
    Images): p. 60
Keystone/Stringer/Hulton Archive/
    Getty Images: p. 64
Mondadori/Getty Images: p. 70
Heinrich Hoffmann/Time Life Pictures/
    Getty Images: p. 85
Photoshot: p. 88
Interfoto: p. 103
Bettmann/Corbis: p. 106
Hulton Archive/Stringer/Getty Images:
    p. 110
Imagno/Hulton Archive/Getty Images:
    p. 117
Imagno/Hulton Archive/Getty Images:
    p. 118
Keystone/Stringer/Hulton Archive/
    Getty Images: p. 121
Universal Images Group/Getty Images:
    p. 124
Hulton Archive/Stringer/Getty Images:
    p. 136

Hulton Archive/Stringer/Getty Images:
    p. 143
Heinrich Hoffmann/Time & Life
    Pictures/Getty Images: p. 152
AFP/Getty Images: p. 156
S&M/ANSA/UIG/Getty Images:
    p. 159
Interfoto: p. 167
Universal History Archive/Getty Images:
    p. 170
Galerie Bilderwelt/Getty Images:
    p. 191
Keystone/Hulton Archive/Getty Images:
    p. 194 top
Heinrich   Hoffmann/Time   &   Life
    Pictures/Getty Images: p. 194 bottom
Photo12/UIG/Getty Images: p. 220
Popperfoto/Getty Images: p. 226
Reg Speller/Hulton Archive/Getty
    Images: p. 233
Central Press/Getty Images: p. 236
Ralph Morse/Time Life Pictures/
    Gy Images: p. 242
Keystone/Hulton Archive/Getty Images:
    p. 246
Heinrich Hoffman/Interfoto: p. 248
Hulton Archive/Getty Image: p. 253
De Agostini Picture Library: p. 256 top
Keystone/Hulton Archive/Getty Images:
    p. 256 bottom
Keystone-France/Gamma-Keystone/
    Getty Images: p. 263
Popperfoto/Getty Images:
    p. 268

The Authors

Simonetta Garibaldi, was born in Genoa in 1970, attended classical high school and then earned her university degree with honors in Modern Literature with a thesis on the history of geographical exploration, *Reinhold Messner: Life as a Challenge*. She has worked in the field of journalism since 1992, contributing to numerous newspapers and periodicals, including the following: *Corriere Mercantile, La Notte, Il Giornale del Popolo di Lugano, Fortune Italia, Quattroruote, La Padania, Storia Illustrata, Master, Yacht Digest, Yacht Capital, Natural, I quaderni di Lifeventuno, Viaggio in Liguria, Mix Magazine, Il Racconto web, Il Domenicale, Fogli*. She was co-author of the following books: *Enciclopedia del Fascismo* (with Luciano Garibaldi), Editrice Portoria, Milan 1999; *Portofino amore mio: mille anni in piazzetta* (with Mario Oriani and Luciano Garibaldi), Orme Editori, Milan 2003; *Colombo*, Vallecchi Editore, Florence 2005 (limited, numbered edition); *Genova e i Mille* (with Luciano Garibaldi), De Ferrari Editore, Genova 2010.

Luciano Garibaldi, was born in Rome in 1936. He has been a journalist since 1957 in Genoa and Milan and has written over 30 history books. Among the most important: *Century of War* (White Star), translated into eight languages, including Chinese; *La pista inglese: chi uccise Mussolini e la Petacci?* (Ares), published in the United States by Enigma Books as *Mussolini: the Secrets of His Death*; *Mussolini e il Professore*; *Le soldatesse di Mussolini*; *Operazione Walkiria: Hitler deve morire*; *La guerra (non) è perduta*; *I Giusti del 25 Aprile*. Garibaldi has also written many books on the 20-year period known as the Years of Lead, when Italy was subject to a wave of terrorism. These include *Brigate Rosse. Per non dimenticare, Nella prigione delle Brigate Rosse*, together with Judge Mario Sossi, and *Mio marito il commissario Calabresi*, written together with the widow of the police commissioner assassinated by the left-wing group Lotta Continua. Forthcoming publications are *O la Croce o la Svastica*, on the conflict between Pope Pius XII and Hitler, and *Gli eroi di Montecassino. Storia dei polacchi che liberarono l'Italia* (Oscar Storia Mondadori).